Notting Hill Editions is an independent British publisher. The company was founded by Tom Kremer (1930–2017), champion of innovation and the man responsible for popularising the Rubik's Cube.

After a successful business career in toy invention Tom decided, at the age of eighty, to fulfil his passion for literature. In a fast-moving digital world Tom's aim was to revive the art of the essay, and to create exceptionally beautiful books that would be lingered over and cherished.

Hailed as 'the shape of things to come', the family-run press brings to print the most surprising thinkers of past and present. In an era of information-overload, these collectible pocket-size books distil ideas that linger in the mind.

Tracey Ullman is an internationally acclaimed producer, writer, actor and dog lover. She is perhaps best known for her series *The Tracey Ullman Show*, which established her as one of primetime's major comic talents. Ullman has received many industry honours including seven Emmys, a Golden Globe and a BAFTA. Her most recent show *Tracey Breaks the News* met with popular success. Her current dog is a mixed breed terrier named Oscar.

Rhian ap Gruffydd is a reportage and portrait photographer. She began her career in the 1980s, when she documented the lives of Bangkok street children. Her passion for using photography as an instigator of social change also led her to photograph the lives of blind children in Penang, Malaysia. Rhian has worked with numerous charities including Comic Relief, where she chronicled the lives of child soldiers in Sierra Leone and Aids orphans in Zambia. Rhian began photographing dogs by chance when she used her client's dog as a stand in for the lighting test. That picture set her off on an incredible journey as an animal photographer.

(www.Gruffpawtraits.com)

ON DOGS

An Anthology

–

Introduced by
Tracey Ullman

Notting Hill Editions

Published in 2019
by Notting Hill Editions Ltd
Mirefoot, Burneside, Kendal, Cumbria LA8 9AB

Series design by FLOK Design, Berlin, Germany
Cover design by Plain Creative, Kendal
Typeset by CB Editions, London

Printed and bound
by Memminger MedienCentrum, Memmingen, Germany

Edited by Rosie Heys

A CIP record for this book is available from the British Library

ISBN 978-1-912559-15-2

www.nottinghilleditions.com

In order to really enjoy a dog, one doesn't merely try
to train him to be semi-human. The point of it is to open
oneself to the possibility of becoming partly a dog.

– Edward Hoagland

Contents

– Introduction –

I have always been mad about dogs. They make me happy. I've had a great variety of dogs in my life – funny dogs, kind dogs, crazy dogs, dopey dogs. A Bichon Frise ate my baby daughter's umbilical cord. It wasn't attached to her at the time, but was carefully stuck inside my baby book along with her hospital ID. I left the book open on the floor to answer the phone and heard a chewing noise. Dogs do awfully odd things and we think nothing of it and carry on feeding them and letting them sleep on pillows beside our heads.

The smartest dog I ever owned was a small mixed breed called Bianca, saved from an infamous high-kill shelter in downtown LA. She was emaciated, bald, and had a bullet lodged between her lung and liver. For one so hard done by she never bore a grudge to humanity or seemed to suffer from PTSD. As soon as I brought her home her behaviour was exemplary. She didn't chew, bark, or pee indoors. Bianca was so poised that you felt that when you had finished reading *The New York Times* you should pass it on to her. And then, oh joy, we discovered she could sing. A soulful vibrato we would coax out of her by playing a didgeridoo I had picked up in Australia. There was a bit of coyote in her, I think. Bianca lived to sixteen and has a special place in my heart. I cried into her fur when I was going through the hardest of times and got such comfort. She was my friend. It is not a lesser love we feel for these animals. Our connection with them is extraordinary.

Serendipity has sometimes brought me the dogs in my life. I went out to buy a chicken one Sunday and saw Millie outside a dog rescue centre. She was the most adorable thing I had ever seen: coal drop eyes, bristly terrier hair that you could mould into a mohawk, a tail that wagged on an angle like a broken coat hanger. She was as desirable to me as a Fabergé egg. I *had* to take her home immediately. On my return, everyone gasped at Millie's cuteness. My husband, who I had feared would reprimand me, lay her on his chest where she promptly fell asleep. He had found his 'spirit animal'.

But who was Millie? Why was she found wandering in downtown Los Angeles? Why was there not a 'Lost' poster on every lamp post? We soon found out. When Millie awoke, she walked woozily into the hallway and started to whimper. The whimpering became louder and increasingly hysterical. Higher and higher it went, until it became a full-throated glass-shattering screech that reverberated through the hallway and the neighbourhood.

'Millie!' I cried, 'What on earth is the matter?'.

She turned, and suddenly the spell was broken. Her coat hanger tail wagged and she was an amiable companion again. And that was Millie, I have never seen such distinct moods in such a small animal. One minute joyful, balancing on her back legs and covering you in kisses, the next launching herself into full attack mode at the gardener, and always returning to the hallway where her role as a master tragedian was played out.

I think mongrels must have an innate ability to attract kind-hearted humans to look after them. Vita Sackville-West wrote about many different dog breeds, but considered the mongrel to be the luckiest. 'He must speak for himself, with those great wistful eyes, as appealing as a lost child. Fortunately for him he is well able to do so. I have been owned by several mongrels in my time, and never have known dogs more capable of falling on their feet.'

A lot of people are adopting dogs from foreign countries nowadays. An online description of a rescue dog in Egypt reads 'Soraya is a street dog whose ten puppies were taken from her and drowned. She has been kicked, beaten, strangled, gassed, and poisoned, and lives near an open sewer scrounging scraps.' A photo shows a hardened canine balancing on three legs amongst rubble. My daughter pointed out that if Soraya were a human, she would be hard as nails, and not someone you would fly over to share your life.

Why are we so soft-hearted when it comes to dogs? I think the reason is quite simple: dogs can't speak. They don't tell you you're ugly, dressed inappropriately, or have bad breath (their own is usually quite terrible). And they offer unconditional love and loyalty, no matter how badly we behave.

I am aware at times that dogs are very dependent on me, and I feel that I should allow them to be dogs rather than furry humans. Several writers in this collection argue that our love for our pets is a selfish one. Charlotte Perkins Gilman writes 'Our love for dogs is often of the basest . . . No live thing can be happy unless it is free to do what it is built for.'

Why should I decide how my dogs should live their life so it is convenient to me? How blithely we drive them to the vet to be neutered and pick them up all woozy and sterile. 'There there, I'll look after you darling, the vet says you'll be calmer now, have no sex drive, and won't run away.' They stare back at you with shaved tummies and cones around their heads to stop them nibbling at their stitches.

When I was in my twenties, I had a Yorkshire terrier named Binky Beaumont, who I treated like a practice baby. A friend of mine made him outfits. He had a 'Hotel Beaumont' bell hop uniform, with gold tasselled epaulettes, and an Elvis cape with jewels and small silk scarves to hand to fans. He repaid me by peeing on me during a photo shoot with the famous photographer Harry Benson. I was doing the splits on a Hollywood hillside – as you do – and he cocked his leg on me. Harry said 'That's the perfect shot!'

Currently I have a dog called Oscar. He is an older mixed breed terrier I adopted when he was about eight. The adoption agency said he had lived with an old man who died and that his daughter had new-born twins and no time for dogs. I liked him immediately and took him to meet my daughter during her lunch hour. He travelled on the tube and hopped on and off escalators with ease. We sat in a coffee shop and he stared for a long time at a businessman eating a muffin. Eventually Oscar reached out and tapped him on the arm with his bristly white paw. It killed me. The man gave him the rest of his muffin.

Oscar and I had things in common: we were both recently bereaved, and we both liked roast chicken and toast – a good starting point.

Oscar is not crazy or funny or dopey and sadly doesn't sing. He carries himself with great dignity and is calm and wise, but if he spots a squirrel he becomes a complete asshole. I would never make him clothes like I did for Binky. I have bought him a coat for colder days and he looks like a nerdy train spotter in it. He flew with me to Italy last summer and behaved impeccably. We walked round Florence in one hundred-degree heat and he had his photo taken with Japanese tourists on the Ponte

Oscar

Vecchio. I'm not sure that Oscar was aware he had left the country, he just knew there was a lot more prosciutto around.

Sometimes I give him a back story. I imagine he was an air raid warden during the London Blitz. He likes to smoke a pipe, wear tartan slippers and listen to the shipping forecast on Radio 4. I think he has conservative views and is a confirmed bachelor.

I will never know what he was like as a puppy and who else he cared for before me and that makes me sad. Does he remember the old man? Does he grieve? Oscar watches the TV and growls when white dogs come on during Crufts Dog Show – he is racist.

At Battersea Dog's Home, I came across this poem engraved on a plaque and it's stayed with me ever since. A dog is not a 'house-dog' or a 'watch-dog' but a friend.

ONE BROWN DOG

The office door closed, dulling the din from the kennels,
'What do you want this dog for?' I was asked austerely,
'House-dog, watch-dog?' I looked at him, gaunt and
Quivering,
Amber eyes searching mine. 'I want him,' I answered,
'To be my friend.' They were satisfied then.
They wrote on the paper,
       One brown dog.
[...]

Joyous, fleet creature, graceful and ardent and golden,
Look at him now, as he skims the green like a swallow,
Or lies relaxed with a loving head on my instep.
'To be my friend,' did I say?
Well, I know what riches of friendship were pledged by the
Three brief words on the Battersea docket –
One brown dog.

by Dorothy Margaret Stuart

There is a profound connection between humankind and dogs that has existed for thousands of years. What began as a mutually beneficial hunting partnership has developed into a deeper emotional attachment. The writers collected within these pages get to the heart of what makes dogs such fantastic companions, despite the occasional mayhem they may cause. This anthology traces the canine's extraordinary journey from working animal to pampered pet.

To be asked to write a foreword for a book about my favourite creature was extremely daunting. Who am I to be the opening act for James Thurber, Virginia Woolf, Will Self and Shakespeare? But then I realised I know as much about dogs as they do. In the eyes of dogs we are all equal, and I know wholeheartedly that no dog would judge me.

I have a few more dogs left in my life. My dream is to die an old lady surrounded by my family, covered in cashmere blankets and lots and lots of dogs. Crispy terriers with coal drop eyes, silky span-iels whose ears I can clasp in my gnarled hands, puppies with warm pink tummies and sweet breath nestling in my neck. At my feet an Irish wolfhound and a portly Labrador who would alert everyone when I am about to breathe my last. I will be, as I have spent most of my life, covered in dog hair, and I will be happy.

Barbara Woodhouse

– *from* The Complete Woodhouse Guide to Dog Training –

Barbara Woodhouse (1910–1988) was the sole woman among sixty men to study veterinary science at Harper Adams Agricultural College in Shropshire, UK. At the age of twenty-four she went to Argentina on a cargo boat, where she gained a stellar reputation for training wild horses. She is best remembered for her almost magical ability to communicate with, and gain the trust of dogs, in the UK television series *Training Dogs the Woodhouse Way*.

The mind of a dog is forever open to take in, by touch, by telepathy, and by talking, the feelings, ideas, emotions and wishes of its owner. That is, if the dog loves its owner. To get through to a dog's mind you don't need a couch and sweet music or probing questions from a psychiatrist. You need hands that on touching the dog send messages of love and sympathy to its brain. You need eyes that tell the dog who watches them what you are feeling towards it, even though it may be hidden from the outside world, and above all you need telepathy so that the dog thinks with you.

These things are not always born in people.

They can be developed as any sense or gift can be developed. That is, providing the person who wishes to develop them is honest in mind, because with animals you cannot cheat; it is useless watching a trainer handling your dog with hatred or fear in your heart, or dislike of all the things she is doing which you think unnecessary or harsh, or both. If you give an order to your dog by word of mouth and are feeling sorry for it inside, you are doomed to failure. Dogs above all creatures love honesty of purpose. If you pat a dog and your fingers are not carrying a loving message you don't deceive the dog.

No one knows why touch is so important. I think probably blind people know more than any of us about the sensitivity of touch; which is why guide dogs are usually so faithful. But the ordinary handler can develop this touch which calms the wild dog, which produces ecstasy in dogs when you caress them, but it has to come through the fingers or face direct from your heart. In every training school the words: 'Praise your dog' are heard constantly; by those words in my school I don't necessarily mean a big hearty pat. I mean a communion of brain and touch. I lay my face alongside that of the dog with its face cupped in my hands, and I sense a deep love and admiration for it passes right through its mind, often in silent communion, for I have already said: 'What a good dog' and clapped my hands to show approval at the end of the exercise.

But a dog needs more than that if you are to get its complete mind in tune with yours. Unhappy are the handlers who think this is all stuff and nonsense. For it makes dogs truly happy. Lots of dogs have to put up with second-best praise, but if you can't let yourself go, you must at least mean what you say when praising. The tone of voice must convey great joy to the dog. It must convey to him that you think him the most wonderful dog on earth, and you must never mind what other people in the school are thinking. Half the trouble in training schools is the natural restraint and reserve that stifles people in public. They cannot forget themselves and abandon themselves to working and praising or correcting the dog.

It is extraordinary how dogs pick up praise straight from your brain almost before you have time to put it into words. A dog's mind is so quick in picking up your thoughts that, as you think them, they enter the dog's mind simultaneously. I have great difficulty in this matter in giving the owners commands in class for the dog obeys my thoughts before my mouth has had time to give the owner the command. I find it extremely difficult to correct a dog for this, although it shouldn't really be obeying me; it should be tuned to its owner who of course doesn't know what I am going to say until I have said it – that is unless the owner is also telepathic.

Eileeen Battersby

– *from* Ordinary Dogs:
A Story of Two Lives –

Writer and chief literary critic of the *Irish Times*, Eileen
Battersby (1958-2018) wrote her second book *Ordinary
Dogs*, from her farm in Co Meath, Ireland. The book is
a moving account of her twenty-year friendship with her
two characterful dogs Bilbo and Frodo. Following her
death, novelist John Banville wrote 'She loved literature
with a passion almost as intense as her love of animals
and the natural world. And she had such a rich sense of
humour, especially when the joke was on her.'

Freedom is seldom experienced by the modern
dog. Consummate browsers, dogs are patient
and methodical, alert to the mysterious potential of
every trace of scent. To watch a relaxed dog investi-
gating a hedgerow or a ditch is a privilege: you are
observing an uninhibited natural scientist of rare
insight at work. It requires patience on the part of
the human and sufficient time for the dog to assess
the immense variety of scents. But most dogs don't
get those chances, not now. The city dog has long
been living a life of confinement. An acquaintance
once assured me that her large Old English Sheep-
dog was 'completely content', living as he did in her
suburban garage with no light and a five-minute

toilet break in the morning and at night. 'It's easier to keep him clean', she added. It was a tragic existence, but it is not that uncommon, although one more usually endured by small dogs. People still aspire to own the large breeds as trophy pets; the pedigree of a dog is often treated with more respect than the actual animal.

The truth is that the best a city dog can hope for are those inadequate morning and evening walks, with perhaps a secure garden to patrol. Roaming the city streets carries more risks than being hit by a car. In the city a stray dog can become the enemy, resorting to theft and, at times, to attack – usually in self-defence. For the urban dog owner, walking his or her confined pet ironically creates a pleasant release for both parties through the dog's need to be exercised, and this duty can offer a lifeline to the human, who also benefits from the walk, although the dog would prefer to explore, to improvise. Being attached by a leash to a human programmed to walk in a straight line can be very frustrating for a dog more inclined to a zigzag approach to exploration. It confuses rivals as well as enemies; only the very best sniffer dog could possibly follow another's browsing trail.

So the city dog gets a regimented walk, is denied any chance of imaginative variation and is accompanied by a human with no appreciation of the wonders of smell and little inclination for meandering digressions. Dogs are improvisers; they don't plan routes.

Yet the all-forgiving dog has a flair for adapting to human limitations. If treated well, they invariably understand or at least accept the life that is given to them. Not that a dog's life is all that much better in today's countryside. Many farmers consider dogs as much a menace as the fox. A farmer near where I live recently bragged about shooting local domestic pets, including a big Labrador who had dared stray about a hundred metres from his owner's gate.

All of this was in my mind as I anticipated the life to come when we began our walks. Eventually Bilbo was fully vaccinated and prepared to experience the world. Then it all began. A leash attached to his collar, by me, aware that it was the first time I had ever done such a thing, and off we went on a bright, cold, January morning. Bilbo tugged like a small husky. As for me, I was not a natural walker: I had always run, cycled or ridden horses, other people's until I had my own. Running with Bilbo was never going to work; a runner is a poor dog walker. We like to run onwards with no diversions. The dog has other ideas. The combination of runner and browsing dog can work in an open field or on an empty beach, but not where there is a chance of a car appearing from the shadows. Bilbo that morning had his head down, and he tugged and gasped, a pack pony on a mission. I followed, careful not to step on him. He had grown bigger; the walking was like a workout for him and it was developing his shoulders. If I tried to jog along with him, he became excited, wheeling about and wrapping the leash around my legs. It was better to walk sedately; I could go running later, alone.

A housewife called to me from her garden. 'She's so cute, like a cuddly toy, what's its name?' It? Cuddly toy? I told her his name and said I was hoping that he would become less toy-like and more of a German Shepherd. I was aware of sounding like an idiot and softened my priggish reply with a smile. Bilbo had other plans, though, and he marched on, neck bizarrely elongated, paws clawing at the ground. I wondered, should I get him a harness? Did they come in such small sizes? He pulled on and there was a ping – his collar snapped and he was gone. Now we *were* running. He darted here and there, enjoying the chase; I ran after him, not as taken as he was by the game because I feared the sudden arrival of a car. Now tired, Bilbo sat down in the middle of the road. He was still a baby and not yet the fluent powerful athlete he would become. He panted, wagging his tail, and then crouched down, tail and bum in the air.

I lifted him up and jogged back to the verge just as a car appeared, I tried looping the leash around his neck but his sled-dog pulling caused the leash to tighten like a noose. He gagged. Back in my arms, he coughed as I carried him home. Dog walking was clearly more complicated than it looked.

J. R. Ackerley

– *from* My Dog Tulip –

J. R. Ackerley (1896–1967) was a British writer and distinguished literary editor. *My Dog Tulip* is a memoir of
Ackerley's profound relationship with his beloved and
ill-behaved German Shepherd dog Tulip, whom he
described as his 'ideal friend'.

T ulip's face perpetually said the same thing,
for with all its perpendicular lines, the tall
ears, the long nose, the black streak down the forehead and the little vertical eyebrow tufts, it was
not merely interrogatory but exclamatory also: it
said both 'What?' and 'What!' Useless to call her
now, she would not budge; I must return to her and
reach my objective by another route; but later I discovered that she would consent to follow me down
these unsavoury roads so long as I reassured her, by
passing the surgeries, that it was not my intention
to enter them. Then she would come, but always
with infinite distaste, crossing the road to make the
widest possible detour and hurrying past the bale-
ful buildings, casting at them every now and then a
repugnant, sidelong glance.

But my disinclination to visit vets was in frequent

conflict with my need to consult them; perplexities of all sorts troubled my ignorant and anxious mind, and not the least of my worries at the time of the encounter with the old woman in Fulham Palace Gardens was that, in spite of the nourishing food I provided, Tulip looked too thin; beneath her sable tunic all her ribs were visible. The distressing word 'Worms' was dropped into my ear by a kind acquaintance, and soon afterwards I decided to take her along to see Miss Canvey, which was the name of the lady vet who had been 'so clever and so kind.' Her surgery was in Parsons Green, and to the kennel-maid who answered the phone I explained, in the apologetic manner which was now habitual to me, that my bitch was very difficult and I would prefer, if convenient, to bring her along out of surgery hours.

Miss Canvey was a short, thickset, young woman with bobbed hair, spectacles and a homely peasant's face. She wore a white overall, not intimidatingly clean, and as she advanced across the large, bare room towards me, I took an impression of calmness and competence. I had spoken sternly to Tulip as we waited, exhorting her to good behaviour for a change, but I had no expectation of any improvement and there was none; she accorded Miss Canvey her usual defiant reception – defiance which became the more empathic the more it was ignored. Miss Canvey approached imperturbably and stood quietly in front of us, looking down at her, while I stumbled through some account of her past and present troubles, punctuated with irritable commands to the dog to pipe down.

'She's like this with everyone,' I said ruefully, 'but as sweet as pie to me. I can't make it out.'

Miss Canvey did not speak, but continued to gaze down at the excited animal. Then she asked:

'What's her name?' I told her. 'Well Tulip, you *are* a noisy girl, aren't you? What's it all about?' and she extended her hand, back foremost. Tulip paused for a moment to sniff it, then, as the hand was moved closer, retreated, barking more violently than ever. How maddening, how intolerable it was that this creature, usually so attentive and obedient to my wishes, should always let me down in public in this stupid way! Suddenly yelling 'Stop it you brute!' I biffed her on the nose. The blow was harder than I intended. Tulip gave a little cry of pain and rubbed her nose with her paw. Then she rose up on her hind legs and gently licked my face.

'I see,' said Miss Canvey promptly. 'You're the trouble.'

'I?' I exclaimed, astonished.

'Just slip her lead through her collar, will you. I'll examine her in another room.'

'Are you sure that will be all right?' I asked anxiously, doing as I was bid.

'Perfectly all right.' And twisting the lead round her strong wrist, she marched firmly out of the room, towing behind her the horrified and struggling Tulip who cast back at me agonised glances as she slid and sprawled across the linoleum. The door closed.

Alone in the surgery I listened apprehensively for sounds – screams from Miss Canvey, cries of pain or rage from Tulip, rushing feet, banging doors – sounds of any sort: none could be reassuring. But the place was as silent as the grave. Then after what seemed an eternity but was only ten minutes, I heard a scuffling in the passage and a few barks, but of a very different timbre; the door opened and Tulip reappeared, this time with Miss Canvey in tow.

'No sign of worms', remarked the latter, dropping the lead. 'She is in excellent condition.'

'How did she behave?' I asked, while Tulip cast herself into my arms and lavished upon me a greeting more suitable in its extravagance to lovers who had been parted for years.

'Good as gold,' said Miss Canvey.

'Did you tie up her nose?'

'Heavens, no! I never do that.'

'But you had help?' I said, gazing mistily at her. Miss Canvey smiled:

'Of course not. She was no trouble. I knew she wouldn't be.'

'How did you know?' I asked humbly

'Well, you learn by experience I suppose. But it isn't difficult to tell a dog's character from its face.

11

Tulip's a good girl, I saw that at once. You're the trouble.'

I sat down.

'Do tell me,' I said.

'Well, she's in love with you, that's obvious. And so life's full of worries for her. She has to protect you to begin with; that's why she's upset when people approach you: I expect she's a bit jealous too. But in order to protect you she's naturally got to be free; that's why she doesn't like other people touching her; she's afraid, you see, that they may take hold of her and deprive her of her freedom to guard you. That's what all the fuss is about, I should say. It's you she's thinking of. But when you're not there, there's nothing for her to do, of course, and no anxiety. Anyone can handle her then. I'm sure. That's all,' she concluded with a smile. 'Dogs aren't difficult to understand. One has to put oneself in their position.'

Miss Canvey could have put herself in any position she wished, for I was already her slave and gazed at her with the veneration with which we behold a saint. I asked her some questions about Tulip's diet, paid the fee – half a crown, so far as I recall, was all that this miracle cost – and took my leave. As I was going, she suddenly said:

'Why do you shout at her?'

'I don't know,' I stammered, rather taken aback. 'She exasperates me sometimes. She doesn't seem to hear what I say.'

'She can hear a pin drop!' said Miss Canvey briefly. 'Look at her ears!' Then on a milder note: 'Try not to. It's bad for her. She's very highly strung. Speak to her quietly; she'll do everything you want in time.'

As we walked away I apologized to Tulip for hitting her on her beautiful nose, and, in my thoughts, for much else besides. In the light of Miss Canvey's interpretation, how infinitely more hideous that abject struggle in the last vet's surgery now seemed, how heroic her conduct, how mean and contemptible mine. I had apologized for her devotion, and then betrayed it. I recollected, with a shudder, how I had held her head still for the approaching trap. I felt very tender towards her.

William Shakespeare

– *from* The Two Gentlemen of Verona –

Shakespeare (1564–1616) often used dogs as metaphors in his plays. In this speech from *The Two Gentleman of Verona*, the comic servant Launce complains that he has often suffered the consequences of his dog's ill-behaviour. Launce has been whipped, put in the stocks, and pilloried, all to save his dog Crab from a worse punishment. He asks 'How many masters would do this for his servant?'

Act II, Scene IV. Under SILVIA'S Window.

Enter LAUNCE with his dog.

LAUNCE. When a man's servant shall play the cur with him, look you, it goes hard: one that I brought up of a puppy; one that I sav'd from drowning, when three or four of his blind brothers and sisters went to it. I have taught him, even as one would say precisely 'Thus I would teach a dog.' I was sent to deliver him as a present to Mistress Silvia from my master; and I came no sooner into the dining-chamber, but he steps me to her trencher and steals her capon's leg. O, 'tis a foul thing when a cur cannot keep himself in all companies! I would have, as one should say, one that takes upon him to be a dog indeed, to be, as it were, a dog at all things. If I had not had more wit than he, to take a fault upon me that he did, I think verily he had been hang'd for't; sure as I live, he had suffer'd for't. You shall judge. He thrusts me himself into the company of three or four gentleman-like dogs under the Duke's table: he had not been there – bless the mark! – a pissing while but all the chamber smelt him. 'Out with the dog!' says one; 'What cur is that?' says another; 'Whip him out!' says the third: 'Hang him up' says the Duke. I, having been acquainted with the smell before, knew it was Crab, and goes me to the fellow that whips the dogs. 'Friend,' quoth I, 'you mean to whip the dog?' 'Ay, marry do I,' quoth he. 'You do him the more wrong,' quoth I; "twas I did the thing you wot of.' He makes me no more ado, but whips me out of the chamber. How many masters would do this for his servant? Nay, I'll be sworn, I have sat in the stock for puddings he hath stol'n, otherwise he had been executed; I have stood on the pillory for geese he hath kill'd, otherwise he had suffer'd for't. Thou think'st not of this now. Nay, I remember the trick you serv'd me when I took my leave of Madam Silvia: Did not I bid thee still mark me and do as I do? When didst thou see me heave up my leg and make water against a gentlewoman's farthingale? Didst thou ever see me do such a trick?

Attila József

– The Dog –

Attila József (1905–1937) was born in Budapest, Hungary, and published his first collection of poetry, *Beauty's Beggar*, aged only seventeen. He became one of the greatest Hungarian poets of the 20th century. József loved deeply and often unrequitedly, a subject he returns to in his poems. He died beneath the wheels of a train aged just thirty-two.

He was so shaggy, sloppy wet,
His coat a yellow flame.
His hunger-trimmed
desire-wasted
sad flanks
sent the cool night breeze
streaming a long way.
He ran and he begged.
Crowded, sighing churches
stood in his eyes
and he scavenged
for breadcrumbs, any old scrap.

I felt sorry for him
as if that poor dog had

crawled out of myself.
I saw in him all
that is mangy in the world.

We go to bed because we have to,
because night puts us to bed,
and we fall asleep
because starvation lulls.
But before dropping off,
as we lie, like the city,
mute under the chill vault
of fatigue and clarity
suddenly he creeps forth
from his daytime hideout
inside us,
that oh so hungry,
muddy, ragged dog
hunting for
god-scraps
god-crumbs.

Translated by John Batki

Dachshund (Long Haired)

Charlotte Perkins Gilman

– *from* On Dogs –

Charlotte Perkins Gilman (1860–1935) was a prominent
American writer, feminist and social reformer. In her radi-
cal and popular manifesto *Women and Economics* (1898),
she argued for economic independence for women. Gilman was also an advocate for reforming the treatment of
domesticated animals. Gilman wrote and published her
own magazine *The Forerunner* in which the following
abridged essay first appeared.

M an's relation to the other beasts has been an
interesting one from the beginning. According to the Hebraic account, he was created master of
all the lower animals, but according to anthropol-
ogy, he has had a long up hill struggle for supremacy.
Of our carnivorous competitors, we have extermi-
nated some, or at least outlived them; with some we
are still at war in frontier regions; and some have
become our friends or servants, as the cat and dog,
cow, horse and sheep.

We have literally made certain animals, as the
Japanese makes his dwarf trees.

The mule is one of our manufactures, ill-tem-
pered and sterile, no doubt unhappy in his hybrid
consciousness, but a useful pulling machine. The

gross and filthy hog is another of our masterpieces. Not content with the beast as God made it, we fell to and altered this edible brother to suit an educated taste. [. . .] In all these conscienceless dealings with living forms, no creature has been more constantly under man's hand than the dog. Their connection is perhaps the earliest of all, dating far back to prehistoric times when there was not so much difference between man and the other brutes.

The hunting savage saw and envied the skill of the hunting dog. The wild dog hunted in packs and so developed the capacity for concerted action, for obedience to signal, and for division of a common victim, which made him more amenable to the new combination than the individualistic feline carnivore. Cheetah, cormorant, hawk – man succeeded in taming and training many creatures to help him hunt, but the dog was most submissive and most serviceable. Perhaps it is owing to the jackal ancestry with which our dog is credited, that he took so kindly to restraint and command, cuffs and kicks and curses; and so man grew to love him. The jackal theory accounts for the presence of the dog most perfectly, for that ingenious beast was always a follower, tagging the lion and tiger for their leftovers of bones and carrion, and when man proved the most successful hunter, he tagged him. He became a creature useful, faithful, utterly submissive; a helpless unresisting humble slave; a thing upon its back with futile paws all waving in the air – this manner of beast appealed to the spirit of primitive man, and the two were united securely. The union holds long after the use has ceased; and the dog lingers on in prolonged survival as a well-beloved rudiment. He is grafted upon humanity as a fixture it appears, though his value lessens with the advance of civilization, and his own health, happiness and dignity lessens in the same proportion. [. . .] So the dog, as a human appendage, seems to have no other explanation than an emotional one; he is a vehicle of expression for the larger creature, a relief to the nerves.

His original service was that of hunter and great was his value when hunting was our chief means of support. When hunting becomes merely a sport, we have the dog still 'useful' in a process which has no use; a sort of toy for grown men in a game the pleasure of which lies in giving full swing to the instincts and passions of our racial infancy. These are crude instincts, brutal passions, which the wise freedom of our later life-processes tend steadily to eliminate, but which men still find pleasure in because it is easier to slip downward than to push up. [. . .]

After the hunting period came the dog's noblest use, in his place as shepherd. To learn to protect his whilom prey, to fight for instead of against a helpless thing, to apply his energy and intelligence to taking care of a creature instead of destroying it, this was splendid progress for the dog. In this work grew his soul as man's grew under the same influence. He had to use new capacities, higher capacities, and had higher pleasure in them. So from mere foxiness he grew to wisdom, developing a broader intelligence in this complex interaction with man as a caretaker and defender. The herd-dog is a noble and healthy creature; and not distinguished for a spaniel-like servility. He obeys, but does not fawn and cringe so much. He knows his power and value.

Then followed long ages of agriculture; and still, on isolated farms, the dog was useful as a guardian, and happy in his usefulness. Free also to some degree, and happy in his freedom. Hunter, shepherd and watch dog, or sled-dog of the snow lands, all these are respectable.

Then comes the city and the pet. Modern civilization is industrial in its main economic features, though still based on agriculture, and, more remotely, on cattle keeping. As that civilization advances, and villages swell and thicken into cities, the dog has less and less of honest place. He has not sufficient ingenuity to assist in manufacture; there is nothing to hunt but an occasional cat; no need to watch or defend, for the policeman guards, and the skilled burglar cares little for a dog.

Each living animal has a mechanism developed through ages of exercise to perform certain acts. If prevented from the use of his natural abilities the creature suffers. To supply his wants, and 'love' him, is not enough. No live thing can be happy unless it is free to do what it is built for.

In a modern industrial community, he has no legitimate activities of his own, and none of ours; on the contrary he holds a position of absolute parasitism, and of more or less injury to us. In seeking to protect ourselves against the dangers incident to dogs in cities, we are forced to add cruel restrictions to canine life. He must be collared, he must be chained, he must be muzzled, he must not be allowed in the places where he would prefer to go, his life becomes increasingly a burden. [. . .]

The city dog is not useful but useless, and in varying degrees expensive and injurious. He is not happy – his manifold diseases prove that conclusively. He has sunk from friend, comrade, helper, servant, to the position of a pet, and it is this position which calls for honest examination. Of what nature is this relation between dog and man? Is it good for him? Is it good for us? It is easy to answer for the dog. Nature's one silent and ceaseless protest against a wrong position is disease. The dog's relation to man, in cities, is so artificial, so devoid of any legitimate use, so full of painful restrictions, that he responds with a black record of man-made ailments.

In our high-handed seizure of the beast's whole life, we have robbed him of freedom in essential natural processes, condemned him to a universal celibacy, and thus introduced him not only to some of the physical disorders of mankind, but some of our vices, as well. The love of man for dogs is not well proven by this general injury. Those who are prepared to honestly defend the dog's place in the city will maintain that he is so developed in his power to love mankind that he derives a greater pleasure from our companionship than pain from all his losses and restrictions.

This is only provable by a fair trial. Let us suppose a case – a work of pure imagination necessarily, because the dog is now so far from nature. Suppose some dogs, living freely together, mating and rearing their puppies happily, with plenty of food and water and exercise. Then suppose a dog sufficiently devoted to a man to leave his freedom for a kennel, collar, and leash; to leave his mate and young for loneliness and strained converse with occasional fellow prisoners; to leave the joy of hunting and the savor of fresh game for tossed table scraps; and his natural exercise for the art of standing on his hind legs, or fetching stones. Do we really think he would do it?

This is all nonsense, of course, for the wild dog does not care for man, and the tame dog does not know freedom. Cut off from man today, he is indeed a miserable wretch, were he to leave his master. From pauper he must become a thief; from slave, a fugitive. He loses all and gains nothing but the freedom of cold and starvation. The modern dog is completely parasitic in his relation to man, and the affection which holds him to us runs exactly parallel with his only means of support.

Love can never be fairly measured when it lies close to self-interest; however deep, submissive, lasting, it is open to the gravest of suspicions. Suppose the dog did not love man – was surly, fierce, and of a haughty, retaliatory spirit. He would meet with treatment severely painful, and presently cease to exist. Watch a stray dog trying to ingratiate himself with a hoped-for master – i.e., feeder and protector. He knows how to place himself with the stronger animal whose care he covets. He is grateful, too, and faithful, sticking staunchly to the hand that feeds him, even if it beats him also. But in spite of all this palpable weight of interest in the love of dogs for man, no one who knows dogs at all can question the sincerity and depth of their devotion.

The power of love developed in the dog by his dependence upon us is something wonderful – a type for man to study. It may be accounted for in origin on purely economic grounds, but it is there as a fact, nevertheless – a capacity for deep and faithful love in the face of neglect and abuse. Yet this very capacity is a doubtful benefit to the dog. Love is a pleasure in its rich expression, and in its full return. To love as much as a dog loves and have only a wet tongue and wagging tail to express it with – and to have one's caresses rather disliked by the beloved object, must be something of a cross. Up springs the loving dog, all aflame with devotion – muddy paws on our clothes, sloppy tongue on our faces – and we bear it awhile if we are good-natured, and then tell him to 'go lie down!' If not good-natured, we will have none of it.

It may well be questioned whether the dog's great love does not give him more pain than pleasure when he has no longer any real avenue of expression. Another element of his distress is in the irritating pressure of the abilities we have so carefully developed in him during his centuries of usefulness, and which find no exercise in his city life. Acting in unison with man so long, he desires in every quivering inch to act so still; and, failing to be used as before, becomes a reservoir of unbalanced energy. He is the engine and man the engineer. He cannot run his own machinery. Hence the nervous, aimless activity when his master takes him out. In running frenziedly around and around he spends this current of energy which has no right expression; a yelping, quivering streak of enthusiasm, he rushes frantically to bring a stick or stone, to relieve the pent-up forces of his unnatural life. Unless we allow full expression to the love and the ability we have developed in the dog, he must suffer deeply in his abortive position. There remains the plea of benefit and pleasure to man–the dog may not like it, but we do. Our gain lies in loving the faithful creature and in enjoying his love. This is so universal a feeling that it requires very conscientious and careful analysis.

How and why do we love dogs? Our love for them is open to condemnation on the spot by its indifference to their comfort, health, and happiness. Do we 'love' creatures which we are content to mutilate, enslave, imprison; whose living bodies we desecrate by breeding them to shapes of artificial ugliness – to such physical discords as are surely doomed to various diseases? What manner of love is this?

[. . .]Our love for dogs is often of the basest. We love to have with us a submissive vehicle for our will, an unresisting recipient of whatever we choose to bestow; and we prize in our weak and selfish hearts the undiscriminating devotion of a beast who takes us at our lowest, and demands nothing – absolutely nothing – in return for his affection.

However cruel, dirty, and degraded a man may be, his dog will love him none the less. We call it 'noble' in the dog, but it has not uplifting influence for the man. Slavish devotion is corrupting to the recipient. An all-forgiving, unexacting love is beneficent when it comes from a superior, as is the mother's love, or in some conceptions of the love of God; but from a base dependent it does not help us, rather leads to contentment in our ignominy. A love which carries neither reverence nor service is little more than sensual indulgence. We do not revere the dog, and he bestows his adoration on the just and unjust alike. We ask no service of the dog in the modern city, and so far from serving, we variously imperil him.

There remains of our 'love' a low-grade residue of selfish expression, usually found in those who are not satisfied in other and more normal lines. A human being who is in satisfactory relation with his own kind; a happy husband or wife; one rich in children and in friends; or one whose heart goes out to the unhappy, the poor, the sick, the criminal – this is not the one who takes a dog to walk in chains. A happy heart does not need solace in a dog's caresses, does not turn to this affectionate quadruped for 'something to love!' And the great sensitive heart which suffers in the pain of others and longs to help and serve, would be too wisely tender to find pleasure in the pitiful, restricted life of a pet dog. We try to still our faint qualms on this subject by explaining that our 'lap-dogs' are so bred to the position that they know no other life nor want it. This is true, and a more ingenious and unscrupulous piece of human selfishness was never exhibited. We have deliberately manufactured a little love-machine for our own emotional satisfaction. Breeding our helpless victims as we would – not as they would – we have slowly bred out of them all larger, freer instincts and abilities, bred them small – bred them hideous – bred them as fantastic whim desired – merely because this large animal likes to have a little one grovelling beside it, the living exponent of his ruthless power.

John Steinbeck

– *from* Travels with Charley –

John Steinbeck (1902–1968) wrote *Travels with Charley* during a three month truck tour in 1962 with his black poodle Charley, through forty American states. Steinbeck named his truck Rocinante, after Don Quixote's horse. In the same year he won the Nobel prize in literature. Steinbeck was an acute and passionate social critic, giving voice to the voiceless in *The Grapes of Wrath* and *Of Mice and Men*.

C hicago was a break in my journey, a resumption of my name, identity, and happy marital status. My wife flew in from the East for her brief visit. I was delighted at the change, back to my known and trusted life – but here I run into a literary difficulty.

Chicago broke my continuity. This is permissible in life but not in writing. So I leave Chicago out, because it is off the line, out of drawing. In my travels, it was pleasant and good; in writing, it would only contribute a disunity.

When that time was over and the good-bys said, I had to go through the same lost loneliness all over again, and it was no less painful than at first. There seemed to be no cure for loneliness save only being alone.

Charley was torn three ways – with anger at me for leaving him, with gladness at the sight of Rocinante, and with pure pride in his appearance. For when Charley is groomed and clipped and washed he is as pleased with himself as is any man with a good tailor or a woman newly patinaed by a beauty parlor, all of whom can believe they are like that clear through. Charley's combed columns of legs were noble things, his cap of silver blue fur was rakish, and he carried the pompon of his tail like the baton of a bandmaster. A wealth of combed and clipped mustache gave him the appearance and attitude of a French rake of the nineteenth century, and incidentally concealed his crooked front teeth. I happen to know what he looks like without the tailoring. One summer when his fur grew matted and mildewed I clipped him to the skin. Under those sturdy towers of legs are spindly shanks, thin and not too straight; with his chest ruff removed one can see the sagging stomach of the middle-aged. But if Charley was aware of his deep-down inadequacy, he gave no sign. If manners maketh man, then manner and grooming maketh poodle. He sat straight and nobly in the seat of Rocinante and he gave me to understand that while forgiveness was not impossible, I would have to work for it.

He is a fraud and I know it. Once when our boys were little and in summer camp we paid them the deadly parent's visit. When we were about to depart, a lady parent told us she had to leave quickly to keep her child from going into hysterics. And with brave but trembling lips she fled blindly, masking her feeling to save her child. The boy watched her go and then with infinite relief went back to his gang and his business, knowing that he too had played the game. And I know for a fact that five minutes after I had left Charley he had found new friends and made his arrangements for his comfort. But one thing Charley did not fake. He was delighted to be travelling again, and for a few days he was an ornament on the trip.

Alice Walker

– Crimes Against Dog –

Alice Walker is an internationally celebrated American writer, poet and activist. She has written several international bestsellers including *The Color Purple* and *The Temple of My Familiar*. She was awarded the Pulitzer Prize in Fiction in 1983 and the National Book Award. 'Crimes Against Dog' comes from her essay collection *We are the Ones We Have Been Waiting For: Inner Light in a Time of Darkness*.

My dog, Marley, was named after the late music shaman, Bob Marley. I never saw or heard him while he was alive, but once I heard his music, everything about him – his voice, his trancelike, holy dancing on stage, his leonine dreadlocks – went straight to my heart. He modeled such devotion to the well-being of humanity that his caring inspired the world; I felt a more sincere individual had probably never lived. Considering his whole life a prayer, and his singing the purest offering, I wanted to say his name every day with admiration and love. Marley has grown up on his music; Bob, leaning on his guitar in a large poster on my living room wall, is regularly pointed out to her as her Spirit Dad.

Marley was born December 19, 1995. She shares a birth sign, Sagittarius, with my mother and several friends and acquaintances. At times I feel surrounded by Sags and enjoy them very much; they are fun to be with, outspoken, passionate, and won't hesitate to try new things. They also like chicken. Marley has all these qualities, though I didn't know that the morning I drove out to the breeder to look at the litter of Labrador Retrievers I was told had arrived.

Crossing the Golden Gate Bridge, a friend and I joked about whether I was in fact ready to settle down enough to have a dog. Who would feed it when I was distracted by work? Where would it stay while I was away on book tours? Had I lined up a reliable vet? I had no idea what would happen. I only knew this friend was about to go away on a journey of unknown length. I would be unbearably lonely for her. I needed a companion on whom to lavish my overflowing, if at times distractible, affection. I needed a dog.

My first thoughts are always about enslavement on entering a place where animals are bred. Force. Captivity. I looked at the black and the chocolate Labs who were Marley's parents and felt sad for them. They looked healthy enough, but who knew whether, left to themselves, they would choose to have litter after litter of offspring? I wondered how painful it was to part with each litter. I spoke to both parents, let them sniff my hand. Take in the quality of my being. I asked permission to look at their young. The mother moved a little away from her brood, all crawling over her blindly feeling for a teat; the father actually looked rather proud. My friend joked about offering him a cigar.

I was proud of myself, too, standing there preparing to choose. In the old days of up to several months before, if I were going to choose an animal from a litter I would have been drawn to the one that seemed the most bumbling, the most clueless, the most un-amused. I saw a couple like that. But on this day, that old switch was not thrown: I realized I was sick of my attraction to the confused. My eyes moved on. They all looked much alike, to tell the truth. From a chocolate mother and a black father there were twelve puppies, six chocolate, six black. I'll never get over this. Why were there none with spots?

I asked the woman selling them, whom I tried not to have Slave Trader thoughts about. She shrugged. They never spot, she said. That's the nature of the purebred Lab. Well, I thought. Mother. Once again doing it just any old way you like. Mother is my favorite name for Nature, God, All-ness.

I settled on a frisky black puppy who seemed to know where she was going – toward a plump middle teat! – and was small enough to fit into my hand. I sometimes wish I had chosen a chocolate puppy; in the Northern California summers the dust wouldn't show as much, but I think about this mostly when Marley rolls in the dirt in an effort to get cool.

After seven weeks I returned alone to pick her up, bereft that my friend had already gone on the road. It didn't feel right to pay money for a living being; I would have been happier working out some sort of exchange. I paid, though, and put Marley in my colorful African market basket before stroking the faces of her wistful-looking parents one last time. In the car, I placed the basket in the front seat next to me. I put on Bob Marley's Exodus CD and baby Marley and I sped away from Babylon. We wound our way back through the winter countryside toward the Golden Gate Bridge and the bracing air of San Francisco. Before we had gone twenty miles, Marley, now about the size of my two fists, had climbed out of the basket and into my lap. From my lap she began journeying up my stomach to my chest. By the time we approached the bridge she'd discovered my dreadlocks and began climbing them. As we rolled into the city she had climbed all the way to the back of my neck and settled herself there between my neck and the headrest. Once there she snoozed.

Of the weeks of training I remember little. Dashing down three flights of stairs in the middle of the night to let her pee outside under the stars. Sitting on a cushion in the kitchen, before dawn, her precious black body in my lap, groggily caressing her after her morning feed. Walking with her zipped up in my parka around and around the park that was opposite our house. Crossing the Golden Gate Bridge on foot, her warm body snug in my arms as I swooned into the view. She grew.

Today she is seven years old and weighs almost ninety pounds. People we encounter on walks always ask whether she's pregnant. No, I reply, she's just fat. But is she really? No matter how carefully I feed her or how often I downsize her meals, she remains large and heavy. And she loves to eat so much that when her rations are diminished, she begs, which I can't stand. This is one of those areas where we've had the most work to do. I've settled it lately by taking her off any slimming diet whatsoever and giving her enough food so that she seems satisfied. I did this after she was diagnosed with breast cancer, had surgery, and I realized I might lose her at any time. I did not want her last days to be spent looking pleadingly at me for an extra morsel of bread. To make up for giving her more food, I resolved to walk her more.

The friend who went away never really returned. Marley and I ceased expecting to see her after about the first year. Marley was an amazing comfort to me. What is it about dogs? I think what I most appreciate in Marley is how swiftly she forgives me. Anything. Was I cool and snooty when I got up this morning? Did I neglect to greet her when I came in from a disturbing movie? Was I a little short on the foodstuffs and did I forget to give her a cube of dried liver? Well. And what about that walk we didn't do and the swim we didn't take and why don't I play ball with her the way I did all last week? And who is this strange person you want me to go off with? It doesn't matter what it is, what crime against Dog I have committed, she always forgives me. She doesn't even appear to think about it. One minute she's noting my odd behavior, the next, if I make a move toward her, she's licking my hand. As if to say, Gosh, I'm so glad you're yourself again, and you're back!

Dogs understand something I was late learning: When we are mean to anyone or any being it is because we are temporarily not ourselves. We're somebody else inhabiting these bodies we think of as us. They recognize this. Ooops, I imagine Marley saying to herself, sniffing my anger, disappointment, or distraction. My mommy's not in there at the moment. I'll just wait until she gets back. I've begun to feel this way more than a little myself. Which is to say, Marley is teaching me how to be more self-forgiving. Sometimes I will say something that hurts a friend's feelings. I will be miserable and almost want to do away with myself. Then I'll think, But that wasn't really the you that protects and loves this friend so much you would never hurt them. That was a you that slipped in because you are sad and depressed about other things: the state of your love life, your health, or the fate of the planet. The you that loves your friend is back now. Welcome her home. Be gentle with her. Tell her you understand. Lick her hand.

Animals teach us decline and mortality. We understand the importance of being able to help our ageing parents or grandparents, or ill and incapacitated relatives and friends, in just this accepting way.

Cats, in particular, teach us to be ourselves, whatever the odds. A cat, except through force, will never do anything that goes against its nature. Nothing seduces it away from itself.

Contemplate ways we can strengthen our resolve to live our lives as who we really are. See the beauty, for instance, in forgoing an 'important' meeting or gala event in favor of a warm fire at home and a restorative nap.

What makes us purr with contentment? Find it and let it, easily, find you.

Dr Temple Grandin and Catherine Johnson

– *from* Animals Make Us Human –

Born in 1947 in the USA, Dr Grandin is Professor of Animal Science at Colorado State University, and was inducted to the American Academy of Arts and Sciences in 2016. Diagnosed autistic as a child, she is an inspirational advocate for the neurologically different, and for the humane treatment of farm animals.

What dogs probably need isn't a substitute pack leader but a substitute parent. I say that because genetically dogs are juvenile wolves, and young wolves live with their parents and siblings.

During evolution dogs went through a process called pedomorphosis, which means that dog puppies stop developing earlier than wolf cubs do. It's a kind of arrested development. That's why dogs – especially purebred dogs – look less 'wolfy' than real wolves. Baby animals have 'baby faces' the same way human babies do. New-born wolf puppies have little snub noses and floppy ears just like new-born dog puppies, but the wolf puppy grows up to have a long, pointy nose and tall, pointy ears. Most dogs grow up to have shorter, snubbier noses than wolves, and a lot of dogs have floppy ears like a puppy's ears, too. Purebreds are especially young-looking. A friend of mine says they have 'toy faces'.

Thanks to some really interesting research done in England, we know that dog facial features and dog behavior generally go together. Dr. Deborah Goodwin and her colleagues found that the more wolfy a breed looks, the more grown wolf behaviors it has. To study the connection between wolfy looks and wolf behaviors, she chose the fifteen most important aggressive and submissive behaviors wolves use to communicate with each other during a conflict, and then observed ten dog breeds to see which breeds expressed which behaviors. Aggressive behaviors included things like growling, teeth baring, 'standing over' (one dog puts its head over the other dog's body), and 'standing erect' (the dog stands as tall as it can, with its back arched and its hackles up). Submissive behaviors were things like muzzle licks, looking away (the submissive dog averts its eyes and very slowly turns its head away), crouching, and the passive submit: where the dog lies on its back and exposes its anogenital area.

Dr. Goodwin found that Siberian huskies, which of the ten breeds look the most like wolves, had all fifteen behaviors, whereas Cavalier King Charles spaniels, which look nothing like wolves, had only two. The correlation between looking like a wolf and acting like a wolf was pretty strong across all ten breeds, with some interesting exceptions. Three of the four gun dogs – cocker spaniels, Labrador retrievers, and golden retrievers – had somewhat more wolfy behaviors than their appearance predicted, and two of the sheepdogs – German shepherds and Shetland sheepdogs – had somewhat fewer wolfy behaviors than their pointy noses and ears predicted. The German shepherd and Shetland sheepdog are probably the exceptions that prove the rule because their facial features were deliberately bred into them starting with shepherding stock. The German shepherd was intentionally bred to look as much like a wolf as possible. Dr. Goodwin says that may mean that once a breed has lost a behavior you can't bring the behavior back just by changing its appearance. So although looks and behavior go together genetically, they can also be separated genetically. She thinks the reason the gun dogs kept as many wolfy behaviors as they did might be because hunting dogs need 'a fuller range of ancestral behavior' to do their job.

Even with the exceptions, the overall order supported her hypothesis:

Cavalier King Charles spaniel:
2 wolf behaviors out of 15
Norfolk terrier: 3 of 15
French bulldog: 4 of 15
Shetland sheepdog: 4 of 15
Cocker spaniel: 6 of 15

Munsterlander: 7 of 15
Labrador retriever: 9 of 15
German shepherd: 11 of 15
Golden retriever: 12 of 15
Siberian husky: 15 of 15

It would be interesting to do Dr. Goodwin's study using mixed-breed dogs. Mutts revert to a somewhat wolfy body form fairly quickly, but do they also get some of the wolfy behaviors back? No one knows.

When you think about dogs being wolves that haven't finished growing up, people who treat their dogs as if they're children might have the right idea after all – although that doesn't necessarily make them good 'dog parents'. Also, people who buy lap dogs and treat them like babies are probably right for at least some of the highly neotenized toy breeds that have retained puppylike behavior. Dr. Goodwin says that a King Charles spaniel never matures mentally beyond the stage of a puppy. It even looks very much like a puppy after it is full grown. I saw an adult Cavalier at the airport once while I was waiting to catch my flight. Everybody was coming up to pet this darling, puppy-like dog.

If dogs need parents, does this mean people should throw out their guidebooks on how important it is to establish themselves as the alpha dog?

I think it depends on the book. Some of the guides have probably been right for the wrong reason. Dog owners do need to be the leader, but not because a dog will become the alpha if they don't. Dog owners need to be the leader the same way parents do. Good parents set limits and teach their kids how to behave nicely, and that's exactly what dogs need, too. Dogs have to learn good manners and their owners have to teach them. When dogs don't have good human parents, they get crazy and out of control and take over the house the same way an undisciplined, spoiled child gets crazy and out of control and takes over the house. It probably doesn't matter whether you think of yourself as the alpha or as the mom or dad so long as you raise your dog right. And because a dog never does grow up mentally, you have to keep on being a good parent and setting limits even after your dog is grown up physically.

One way or another, the human has to be in charge. Whether you think of yourself as mom, dad, or pack leader probably doesn't matter as long as you're handling your dog right.

Yorkshire Terrier Cross

Vita Sackville-West

– The Mongrel –

English writer, poet and gardener Vita Sackville-West (1892-1962) had many dogs, including a Saluki gifted to her by Gertrude Bell. Named Zurcha, she was described by Sackville-West as both 'a marvel of elegance' and 'the dullest dog I ever owned'. Sackville-West and her lover Virginia Woolf communicated in letters adopting the character of an imaginary dog named Potto, whose death of a broken heart Woolf conveyed to Sackville-West when their love affair ended. The following piece first appeared in Sackville-West's book *Faces: Profiles of Dogs*.

Alas, we honour him with no history, no pedigree. He must speak for himself, with those great wistful eyes, as appealing as a lost child. Fortunately for him he is well able to do so. I have owned, or been owned by, several mongrels in my time, and never have known dogs more capable of falling on their feet. Some of them have been pi-dogs; one made her way into my house in Constantinople, and, too savage to be ejected, gave birth to a litter of puppies on the drawing-room sofa; another dreadful little object collected me in the bazaar of Teheran, followed me home, and took complete possession. The faces of the Persian servants when I made them give him a bath, badly needed, were worth seeing.

Then there was Micky, who had a dash of Irish terrier in him. I think Micky must be the only dog who has openly walked ashore off a battleship on to English soil without being intercepted and clapped into quarantine. I had left him behind in Turkey, when, unable to return myself, owing to the outbreak of war, the Ambassador who detested dogs but to whom I remain eternally grateful brought him home to me on a string. Micky it was, too, who, falling through a skylight when he ought by all rules to have been killed, contrived to land on a bed – though that was perhaps due to good luck rather than good management.

The worst of mongrels is that they are apt to be so very plain. Micky himself was no beauty. Good breeding tells. One has noticed the extreme ungainliness of dogs lying about the streets of foreign villages, and has been thankful that the proportions of these mistakes is not so high in Britain. But for sheer urchin wit and resourcefulness the mongrel can be hard to beat, only unfortunately when tempted to acquire an irresistible puppy one is seldom aware of its lineage, immediate or remote, and thus cannot estimate what characteristics it is likely to develop in later life. Will it have a bit of sheep-dog in it, and proudly, but inconveniently bring one a flock of sheep belonging to somebody else? Will it have a bit of terrier, and have to be dragged backwards by its tail out of a rabbit-hole? Or will it be merely a small scavenger, preferring unspeakable filth to the nice bowl we painstakingly provide? One must take one's chance, and in some cases one's life is no longer likely to be one's own.

George Catlin

– *from* Illustrations of the Manners, Customs, and Condition of the North American Indians –

George Catlin (1796–1872) was an American painter and author. He specialised in portraits of American Indians and travelled extensively among the native peoples of the Americas. In his book about North American Indians, published in 1856, the author notes that it was 'Written during eight years of travel and adventure among the wildest and most remarkable tribes now existing.'

T he dog, amongst all Indian tribes, is more esteemed and more valued than amongst any part of the civilized world; the Indian who has more time to devote to his company, and whose untutored mind more nearly assimilates to that of his faithful servant, keeps him closer company, and draws him nearer to his heart. They hunt together and are equal sharers in the chase. Their bed is one and on the rocks and on their coat of arms they carve his image as the symbol of fidelity. Yet, with all of these, the Indian will end his affection with this faithful fol-lower, and with tears in his eyes, offer him as a sacri-fice to seal the pledge he has made to man; because a feast of venison or of buffalo meat is what is due to everyone and consequently has no meaning.

I have sat at many of these feasts and never could but appreciate the moral solemnity of them. I have seen the master take the bowl with the head of his beloved dog and descant on its former affection with tears in his eyes. At the feast I'm describing, each of us tasted a little of the meat, and passed the dishes on to the Indians who soon demolished everything that they contained. We all agreed that the meat was well cooked, and seemed to be well flavored and palatable; and no doubt, could have been eaten with good relish had we been ignorant of the nature of the food we were eating.

Charles Dickens

– *from* Oliver Twist –

Charles Dickens (1812–1870) characterised several dogs
in his novels. Bullseye is Dickens' meanest-natured dog,
and shares the violent tendencies of his owner Sikes. But
even Bullseye is loyal to the last, following his master to
his death.

I n the obscure parlour of a low public-house, in
the filthiest part of Little Saffron Hill; a dark and
gloomy den, where a flaring gas-light burnt all day in
the winter-time; and where no ray of sun ever shone
in the summer: there sat, brooding over a little pewter measure and a small glass, strongly impregnated
with the smell of liquor, a man in a velveteen coat,
drab shorts, half-boots and stockings, whom even
by that dim light no experienced agent of the police
would have hesitated to recognise as Mr. William
Sikes. At his feet, sat a white-coated, red-eyed dog;
who occupied himself, alternately, in winking at his
master with both eyes at the same time; and in licking a large, fresh cut on one side of his mouth, which
appeared to be the result of some recent conflict.

'Keep quiet, you warmint! Keep quiet!' said Mr.
Sikes, suddenly breaking silence. Whether his medi-

tations were so intense as to be disturbed by the dog's winking, or whether his feelings were so wrought upon by his reflections that they required all the relief derivable from kicking an unoffending animal to allay them, is matter for argument and considera-tion. Whatever was the cause, the effect was a kick and a curse, bestowed upon the dog simultaneously.

Dogs are not generally apt to revenge injuries inflicted upon them by their masters; but Mr. Sikes's dog, having faults of temper in common with his owner, and labouring, perhaps, at this moment, under a powerful sense of injury, made no more ado but at once fixed his teeth in one of the half-boots. Having given it a hearty shake, he retired, growl-ing, under a form; just escaping the pewter measure which Mr. Sikes levelled at his head.

'You would, would you?' said Sikes, seizing the poker in one hand, and deliberately opening with the other a large clasp-knife, which he drew from his pocket. 'Come here, you born devil! Come here! D'ye hear?'

The dog no doubt heard; because Mr. Sikes spoke in the very harshest key of a very harsh voice; but, appearing to entertain some unaccountable objec-tion to having his throat cut, he remained where he was, and growled more fiercely than before: at the same time grasping the end of the poker between his teeth, and biting at it like a wild beast.

This resistance only infuriated Mr. Sikes the

more; who, dropping on his knees, began to assail the animal most furiously. The dog jumped from right to left, and from left to right; snapping, growling, and barking; the man thrust and swore, and struck and blasphemed; and the struggle was reaching a most critical point for one or other; when, the door suddenly opening, the dog darted out: leaving Bill Sikes with the poker and the clasp-knife in his hands.

There must always be two parties to a quarrel, says the old adage. Mr. Sikes, being disappointed of the dog's participation, at once transferred his share in the quarrel to the new comer.

'What the devil do you come in between me and my dog for?' said Sikes, with a fierce gesture.

'I didn't know, my dear, I didn't know,' replied Fagin, humbly; for the Jew was the new comer.

'Didn't know, you white-livered thief!' growled Sikes. 'Couldn't you hear the noise?'

'Not a sound of it, as I'm a living man, Bill,' replied the Jew.

'Oh no! You hear nothing, you don't,' retorted Sikes with a fierce sneer. 'Sneaking in and out, so as nobody hears how you come or go! I wish you had been the dog, Fagin, half a minute ago.'

'Why?' inquired the Jew with a forced smile.

''Cause the government, as cares for the lives of such men as you, as haven't half the pluck of curs, lets a man kill a dog how he likes,' replied Sikes, shutting up the knife with a very expressive look; 'that's why.'

Miranda Hart

– *from* Peggy & Me –

Miranda Hart is an award-winning British writer, come-
dian and actress. She is best known for her hugely successful sitcom *Miranda*. *Peggy & Me* charts the story of
her life since getting a Shih-Tzu Bichon Frise cross puppy
named Peggy.

D OGS ARE BETTER THAN CATS.
There, I've said it. Those who are now
leaving the room in horror, cat in hand, please come
back, for I have plenty more to say on the subject.
I wouldn't dream of making such a statement and
then vanishing in a puff of smoke; I must back up
my bold assertion, and I'd like to devote this, what
I will call, Interlude, to arguing my case with all the
bounce and vim of a beagle who's just spied a joint
of lamb. We shall now launch into Miranda's Bold
and Bouncy Argument As to Why Dogs Are Better
Than Cats. Such fun.

Let's kick off – perhaps a little unfairly – with
a look at the Nutty Cat Owners. I would argue that
the sheer number of mad-as-a-brush cat owners is all
the evidence one needs of the essential superiority of
dogs. Of course, I'm well aware that dog ownership

can drive a person mildly crackers (please refer to my earlier musings on the cross-section of Extreme Dog Owners to be found in my local park), and I'm also aware that I myself am at risk of becoming a crazy dog owner, absolutely yes (I have written a WHOLE BOOK about my dear dog, for heaven's sake) – but I'd argue that Cat Nutters are approximately 1,473 per cent nuttier than your average Dog Nutter (all statistics in this book are 87.5 per cent made up). Reasons to follow. I think this calls for a list. Who doesn't love a little list?

1. Anthropomorphizing and humanizing cats. This is of course the prime manifestation of most animal related nuttiness, but also the one that gives an enormous amount of joy to us owners. And it officially appears so, so much madder with a cat than a dog. For example… oh, hold on, I think there's going to be a list within a list. Well, this is TREMENDOUS.

i. Costumes. If you put, say, a little Spiderman costume on a dog to protect it from the rain it looks rather natty. Dapper. Happy to be togged up and hoping it's off to a party. Put an identical costume on a cat and it looks like a rugby player who's passed out on a stag night and woken up to find his friends have dressed him in a French Maid's outfit. The cat looks, in short, abused.

ii. Handbags. If you put a dog in a handbag (by which I mean something like a Chihuahua in a Burberry shoulder bag, not trying to stuff an Alsatian into a rucksack) it looks fine. Rather impressive, even. Smart. Kardashian-esque. If you were to put a cat in a bag and bring it to work, you'd look like the very maddest of the mad. You might as well wear a wetsuit to your Zumba class. Or marry your photocopier.

iii. The way you interact with your pet. If you were to look at your dog and say, 'Buttons the Dog looks sad. Would you like a cuddle, Buttons?' you'd be thought of as a caring pet owner. If you were to do exactly the same to a cat, you'd be thought of as a merry lunatic, most likely projecting your own emotions on to the poor blank animal in the absence of any meaningful human contact. And I think we must all be honest about the vast difference between looking into the eyes of a cat, and the eyes of a dog. If, and please allow me a moment of poetry here, if a dog's eyes are like a fast-moving film reel of feelings, all of them sincere, most of them extreme (Devastation! Love! Hope! JOY! Devastation! LOVE!), then staring into a cat's eyes is like staring into a still oily puddle which may or may not turn out to conceal a bottomless pit. Unfathomable. Mysterious. Blank. At very best, a cat's eyes are those of that girl in your class at school, the one who was so effortlessly beautiful and chic that she didn't ever have to bother being anything else. Life to her, was just one big staring contest, and she always won. Well, that's cats for you.

iv. Leads. When you put a lead on a dog, it's normal. A dog is meant to be attached to a human via a lead. It is an entirely natural state of affairs. Put a lead on a cat, and you might just as well whack on a T-shirt bearing the slogan 'I AM A RAMBLING ECCENTRIC, PLEASE GIVE ME A WIDE BERTH OR I WILL COME TO YOU WITH MY WEIRD CAT ON A STRING.'

v. Shows. Ever wonder why there isn't a Crufts for cats? Thought not. Because we all know that Crufts for cats would be completely knockout, stone-cold mental. Fact. Imagine trying to train a cat to go up and down a seesaw and in and out of poles. It would stare at you as if saying, 'Piss off, I'm late for *Newsnight.*' Plus, you'd be back at needing to put a cat on a lead.

Now, if we can interlude within the Interlude – I know, I don't want to confuse you, especially as I have just listed within a list, but try and keep up, MDRC, I can't help being a literary maverick – I need to nip those of you asking 'yes, but who puts a cat on a lead?' in the bud. For I have witnessed this event, twice. Once on a pavement in a busy shopping street in Chiswick, West London. A woman brazenly walking a cat on a colourful ribbon as if it were perfectly normal (please note, a ribbon – Chiswick is frightfully middle-class, no pieces of string here). However confidently this woman walked her cat on a ribbon, she looked CERTIFIABLE. There are a few – and only a very few, I'm afraid – people who can get away with this sort of thing. I would imagine Helena Bonham-Carter could get away with it. And also maybe Grayson Perry.

Generally Americans can get away with cats on leads far better, which brings me to my second cat-on-lead sighting: a beautiful lady out walking some kind of pedigree puss in New York's Central Park. She seemed to carry it – and her leopard-print leggings and matching jacket, hat, shoes, socks and velveteen scrunchie – off rather well. But I think we can chalk that up as one of the many things Americans can do which British people somehow can't.

Elizabeth Cleghorn Gaskell

– *from* The Life of Charlotte Bronte –

Mrs Gaskell (1810–1865) was a close friend of Charlotte Bronte, and the two corresponded frequently until
Charlotte's death in 1855. Mrs Gaskell's biography of
Charlotte Bronte was published in 1857 to immediate acclaim. In this passage she relates how Charlotte
took inspiration from her late sister Emily. Gaskell was
a Unitarian – a progressive and egalitarian faith which
advocates compassion and respect for all animals.

T he feeling, which in Charlotte partook of
something of the nature of an affection, was,
with Emily, more of a passion. Someone speaking of her to me, in a careless kind of strength of
expression, said, 'she never showed regard to any
human creature; all her love was reserved for animals.' The helplessness of an animal was its pass-
port to Charlotte's heart; the fierce, wild, intractabil-
ity of its nature was what often recommended it to
Emily. Speaking of her dead sister, the former told
me that from her many traits in Shirley's character
were taken; her way of sitting on the rug reading,
with her arm round her rough bull-dog's neck; her
calling to a strange dog, running past, with hanging
head and lolling tongue, to give it a merciful draught

of water, its maddened snap at her, her nobly stern presence of mind, going right into the kitchen, and taking up one of Tabby's red-hot Italian irons to sear the bitten place, and telling no one, till the danger was well-nigh over, for fear of the terrors that might beset their weaker minds.

All this, looked upon as a well-invented fiction in 'Shirley', was written down by Charlotte with streaming eyes; it was the literal true account of what Emily had done. The same tawny bull-dog (with his 'strangled whistle'), called 'Tartar' in 'Shirley', was 'Keeper' in Haworth parsonage; a gift to Emily. With the gift came a warning. Keeper was faithful to the depths of his nature as long as he was with friends; but he who struck him with a stick or whip, roused the relentless nature of the brute, who flew at his throat forthwith, and held him there till one or the other was at the point of death.

Now Keeper's household fault was this. He loved to steal upstairs, and stretch his square, tawny limbs, on the comfortable beds, covered over with delicate white counterpanes. But the cleanliness of the parsonage arrangements was perfect; and this habit of Keeper's was so objectionable, that Emily, in reply to Tabby's remonstrances, declared that, if he was found again transgressing, she herself, in defiance of warning and his well-known ferocity of nature, would beat him so severely that he would never offend again.

In the gathering dusk of an autumn evening, Tabby came, half-triumphantly, half-tremblingly, but in great wrath, to tell Emily that Keeper was lying on the best bed, in drowsy voluptuousness. Charlotte saw Emily's whitening face, and set mouth, but dared not speak to interfere; no one dared when Emily's eyes glowed in that manner out of the paleness of her face, and when her lips were so compressed into stone. She went upstairs, and Tabby and Charlotte stood in the gloomy passage below, full of the dark shadows of coming night.

Down-stairs came Emily, dragging after her the unwilling Keeper, his hind legs set in a heavy attitude of resistance, held by the 'scuft of his neck', but growling low and savagely all the time. The watchers would fain have spoken, but durst not, for fear of taking off Emily's attention, and causing her to avert her head for a moment from the enraged brute. She let him go, planted in a dark corner at the bottom of the stairs; no time was there to fetch stick or rod, for fear of the strangling clutch at her throat – her bare clenched fist struck against his red fierce eyes, before he had time to make his spring, and, in the language of the turf, she 'punished him' till his eyes were swelled up, and the half-blind, stupefied beast was led to his accustomed lair, to have his swollen head fomented and cared for by the very Emily herself.

The generous dog owed her no grudge; he loved her dearly ever after; he walked first among the mourners to her funeral; he slept moaning for nights at the door of her empty room, and never, so to speak, rejoiced, dog fashion, after her death. He, in his turn, was mourned over by the surviving sister. Let us somehow hope, in half Red Indian creed, that he follows Emily now; and, when he rests, sleeps on some soft white bed of dreams, unpunished when he awakens to the life of the land of shadows.

Pug

Kathryn Hughes

– Our Long Obsession with Canine Design –

Professor Kathryn Hughes is an academic historian and literary critic who specialises in Victorian culture. The Victorians first began to catalogue canine blood lines and list the ideal attributes for breeds as part of a growing enthusiasm for dog shows.

'Why are mongrels a dying breed?' Jilly Cooper wondered out loud in 2013. She might equally have asked 'Whatever happened to pedigrees?' She was referring to the fact that the dogs you meet these days are seldom pure-bred or mutt, but tongue-twisting mash-ups: labdradoodle, puggle, cavapoo, zuchon, beaglier. The emergence of these artful hybrids in recent years is the result of the marketplace's demand for an animal designed with human needs in mind: loyal but not clingy, confident yet chilled, fluffy as a puffball but mercifully inclined to hang on to its own hair. And exactly the right size to fit into your car.

Dogs, then, are largely human-made manufactures, their changing shape and proliferating forms the consequence of fantasy, hope and greed (a good crossbreed with all its papers now goes for as much as its pedigreed parents). Selective breeding is how it's done, the careful matching of mates in order to produce puppies with exactly the desired characteristics. It's both incredibly simple – dogs are generally delighted with whatever blind date you've set up for them – and profoundly powerful. For within just a few generations, and bear in mind that a dog generation may be as little as six months, you can change the shape of a snout or tame a nasty temper. Within a few more generations you could, in theory, have invented a whole new breed.

In *The Invention of the Modern Dog: Breed and Blood in Victorian Britain* by Michael Worboys, Julie-Marie Strange and Neil Pemberton, three leading historians of science explore the origins of what they call the 'modern' dog. For millennia, canine companions were roughly sorted into types suited for certain tasks. There were big dogs to pull people out of the snow and little dogs to turn the spit, medium-sized dogs to run after sheep and 'toy' dogs to sit on ladies' laps. But with the dawning of the 19th century came a new desire to count, measure, regulate and, above all, improve the natural world. Drawing on the expertise of livestock farmers who had worked out how to produce fluffier sheep, milkier cows and porkier pigs, country gentlemen set about tinkering with their sporting dogs. Spaniels, beagles and retrievers were refined and defined into stable categories that could be guaranteed to breed 'true'. By cleaning up the bloodlines, every new pup would henceforth be an exact copy of its parents.

At the same time there was another set of people who had skin in the dog-breeding game. They comprised the 'Fancy', a loose grouping of urban working-class men who traded dogs for profit. Often operating out of pubs and barber shops, the Fancy was interested in spectacle and show. It liked pretty dogs, ratting dogs, dogs with a bit of pep to them. Infuriated by the way the country gents on judging panels kept giving gongs to their friends and refusing to say why, the Fancy insisted on coming up with a standardised set of 'points' for each breed against which an individual animal might be objectively assessed. Now there were earnest discussions and brisk disagreements about the correct angle of an ear or the desired curl of a tail.

All this sounds sensible. But the Fancy started taking things too far in its scramble to win prizes and make trades. Intense overbreeding resulted in bulldogs that looked like monstrous toads, bloodhounds so slobbery they could barely get their food down, and toy dogs that were nothing but 'goggle-eyed abortions'. What was needed, huffed the gentlemen, were competitions that moved away from the beauty pageant and towards the field trial. Until you'd seen a dog in its natural environment, which is to say tearing round a muddy meadow in a thick drizzle, you couldn't begin to form an opinion on whether or not it was up to snuff.

Tempers started to fray to the point where, in 1880, one breeder sued the newspapers for libelling his prizewinning bloodhound. The case went on for two days and involved thirteen expert witnesses lining up to give their opinion on whether it was fair to describe Napier as 'slack loined'. Increasingly, though, such parochial bickerings were filtered through the more general preoccupations of the day. By the 1890s, there was plenty of xenophobic chatter about how canine 'alien immigration' – all those dachshunds and schipperkes flooding in from the continent – was causing 'Dogdom's Deterioration'. Miscegenation was blamed, too, for a certain lowering of the doggy moral tone: a pedigree bitch who had an accidental mating with a mongrel hadn't simply spoiled a single litter, she had ruined her womb for ever. From now on, all her puppies, no matter how well bred their sire, would bear the indelible stain of their mother's sluttishness.

Father Mark Osborne

– Dogs in Heaven –

The Rev'd Mark Osborne BA MTh was born in 1967, and raised in a vicarage with rabbits, cats, chickens and a dog called Cadbury. Trained and ordained for the priesthood in Yorkshire, he served from 2001 at St John's, Fulham Broadway in London, and in 2018 became the Chaplain of St George's, Paris, which is part of the Church of England's Diocese of Gibraltar in Europe.

Crufts and a myriad of animal charities go to show that the British are mad about animals. But for me, a vicar, it's Dorothy Gurney's poem, herself brought up by and then marrying a vicar, that explains why my parents always buried our family pets in the garden.

> The kiss of the sun for pardon,
> The song of the birds for mirth,
> One is nearer God's Heart in a garden
> Than anywhere else on Earth.

We want our pets and God to go together. Lots of people tell me passionately that 'if there are no dogs/cats/pets in heaven I don't want to go there!' Why should we contemplate separating ourselves from the unconditional acceptance, warm snuggles and happy times that our pets provide? Our pets are so happy being themselves they teach us to live in the moment: heaven is a warm dog snoozing by your side, a cat stretched out in a bar of sunlight. Heaven is the definition of bliss and bliss has got to include the things that make us happy without hurting anyone.

As the Bible is written from the perspective of God's dealings with humans it's not very helpful about pets. It seems we're in an unusual bit of human history with the time, money and space to have dogs and cats alongside us and treated almost as equals in our lives. When I got a dog who made me a better person I realised I wanted her to be more than a collection of atoms randomly put together in a morally purposeless universe! I wanted to believe God made her and me for eternity.

Did you know there's more to dying than heaven? A vicar friend pointed out that at the end of the Christian story God remakes all of Creation. It's a bit like heaven but the end version. Though the remaking is about abolishing death, disease and the scars that humans inflict on each other, a saint Anselm of Canterbury argued that God is bigger than anything we can imagine. So if we can imagine God doing something more loving than the original story then the problem lies with the story. Can I imagine a new Creation with me and a being who loves, even if it's not only food and cuddles but my unwashed socks too? yup! So it makes sense to say that God is perfectly happy to have dogs in heaven!

When her time came, Maud, aka 'The dog-child', the 'Maudster', the 'Oblate Sphere', 'Sweet-pea' (more marrow fat actually), 'Fat-one', 'She Who Is Obeyed', etc. skipped over the Rainbow Bridge to the happy dog place to await the remaking of all Creation. There she can be fully loving and loved, and I can hope to join her. She taught me profound truths in her fourteen years: you can never be too fat or too wrinkly to be loved; sitting on people's feet doesn't necessarily win people over; there's always, always, room for more; and being in contact with humans – there's nothing better. The flat was very quiet that night . . .

Alexandre Dumas

– *from* Mary Stuart 1587 –

Alexandre Dumas (1802–1870) was born in France, the
grandson of a Haitian slave and a French nobleman. A
prolific author and playwright, his works include *The
Three Musketeers* and *The Man in the Iron Mask*. In
his account of the life of Mary Stuart, Queen of Scots,
Dumas tells how when the poet Chatelard hid beneath
the Queen's bed, intent on 'seduction', Mary's Maltese
terrier barked the alarm and saved her; the dog stayed
with the Queen, even to her execution, her blood stain-
ing his white coat red.

T he queen's servants had rushed upon the scaf-
fold, picking up the book of Hours and the
crucifix as relics; and Jeanne Kennedy, remember-
ing the little dog who had come to his mistress,
looked about for him on all sides, seeking him and
calling him, but she sought and called in vain. He
had disappeared.

At that moment, as one of the executioners was
untying the queen's garters, which were of blue satin
embroidered in silver, he saw the poor little animal,
which had hidden in her petticoat, and which he was
obliged to bring out by force; then, having escaped
from his hands, it took refuge between the queen's

shoulders and her head, which the executioner had laid down near the trunk. Jeanne took him then, in spite of his howls, and carried him away, covered with blood; for everyone had just been ordered to leave the hall. Bourgoin and Gervais stayed behind, entreating Sir Amyas Paulet to let them take the queen's heart, that they might carry it to France, as they had promised her; but they were harshly refused and pushed out of the hall, of which all the doors were closed, and there remained only the executioner and the corpse.

Wisława Szymborska

– Monologue of a Dog
Ensnared in History –

Wisława Szymborska (1923–2012) was born in Poland,
and lived most of her life under communist dictatorship.
Her first collections of poetry fell to the censors for not
conforming to the communist ideology. In 1996 she won
the Nobel prize for literature.

There are dogs and dogs. I was among the
     chosen.
I had good papers and wolf's blood in my veins.
I lived upon the heights inhaling the odors of views:
meadows in sunlight, spruces after rain,
and clumps of earth beneath the snow.

I had a decent home and people on call,
I was fed, washed, groomed,
and taken for lovely strolls.
Respectfully, though, and comme il faut.
They all knew full well whose dog I was.

Any lousy mutt can have a master.
Take care, though – beware comparisons.
My master was a breed apart.
He had a splendid herd that trailed his every step

and fixed its eyes on him in fearful awe.
For me they always had smiles,
with envy poorly hidden.
Since only I had the right
to greet him with nimble leaps,
only I could say good-bye by worrying his trousers
with my teeth.
Only I was permitted
to receive scratching and stroking
with my head laid in his lap.
Only I could feign sleep
while he bent over me to whisper something.

He raged at others often, loudly.
He snarled, barked,
raced from wall to wall.
I suspect he liked only me
and nobody else, ever.

I also had responsibilities: waiting, trusting.
Since he would turn up briefly, and then vanish.
What kept him down there in the lowlands, I don't
know.
I guessed, though, it must be pressing business,
at least as pressing
as my battle with the cats
and everything that moves for no good reason.

There's fate and fate. Mine changed abruptly.

One spring came
and he wasn't there.
All hell broke loose at home.
Suitcases, chests, trunks crammed into cars.
The wheels squealed tearing downhill
and fell silent round the bend.

On the terrace scraps and tatters flamed,
yellow shirts, armbands with black emblems
and lots and lots of battered cartons
with little banners tumbling out.

I tossed and turned in this whirlwind,
more amazed than peeved.
I felt unfriendly glances on my fur.
As if I were a dog without a master,
some pushy stray
chased downstairs with a broom.

Someone tore my silver-trimmed collar off,
someone kicked my bowl, empty for days.
Then someone else, driving away,
leaned out from the car
and shot me twice.

He couldn't even shoot straight,
since I died for a long time, in pain,
to the buzz of impertinent flies.
I, the dog of my master.

David Sedaris

– The Youth in Asia –

Author, essayist and playwright David Sedaris is one
of America's pre-eminent humour writers. He is the
author of dozens of books including B*arrel Fever* and
Let's Explore Diabetes with Owls. Sedaris' original radio
pieces can often be heard on the public radio show *This
American Life*, on which this story was aired. Sedaris
asks to what degree can a beloved pet be replaced when
it dies?

'That's it,' my mother said after having Sadie put
to sleep. 'My cat days are over.'

In the early sixties, during what my mother
referred to as the 'tail end of the Lassie years,' my parents were given two collies they named Rastus and
Duchess. We were living in upstate New York, out in
the country, and the dogs were free to race through
the forest. They napped in meadows and stood knee-
deep in frigid streams, co-stars in their own private
dog-food commercial. According to our father, anyone could tell that the two of them were in love.

Late one evening, while lying on a blanket in
the garage, Duchess gave birth to a litter of slick,
potato-sized puppies. When it looked as though one

of them had died, our mother placed the creature in a casserole dish and popped it into the oven, like the witch in *Hansel and Gretel*.

'Oh, keep your shirts on,' she said. 'It's only set on 200. I'm not baking anyone; this is just to keep him warm.'

The heat revived the sick puppy and left us believing our mother was capable of resurrecting the dead.

Faced with the responsibilities of fatherhood, Rastus took off. The puppies were given away, and we moved south, where the heat and humidity worked against a collie's best interests. Duchess's once beautiful coat now hung in ragged patches. Age set in and she limped about the house, clearing rooms with her suffocating farts. When finally, full of worms, she collapsed in the ravine beside our house, we re-evaluated our mother's healing powers. The entire animal kingdom was beyond her scope; apparently, she could resurrect only the cute dead.

The oven trick was performed on half a dozen peakish hamsters but failed to work on my first guinea pig, who died after eating a couple of cigarettes and an entire pack of matches.

'Don't take it too hard,' my mother said, removing her oven mitts. 'The world is full of guinea pigs. You can get another one tomorrow.'

Eulogies always tended to be brief, our motto being 'Another day, another collar.'

A short time after Duchess died, our father

came home with a German shepherd puppy. For reasons that were never explained, the privilege of naming the dog went to a friend of my older sister's, a fourteen-year-old girl named Cindy. She was studying German at the time, and after carefully examining the puppy and weighing it with her hands, she announced it would be called Madchen, which apparently meant 'girl' to the Volks back in the Vaterland. We weren't wild about the name but considered ourselves lucky that Cindy wasn't studying one of the harder-to-pronounce Asian languages.

When she was six, Madchen was killed by a car. Her food was still in the bowl when our father brought home an identical German shepherd, whom the same Cindy thoughtfully christened Madchen Two. This tag-team progression was disconcerting, especially for the new dog, who was expected to possess both the knowledge and the personality of her predecessor.

'Madchen One would never have wet the floor like that,' my father would scold, and the dog would sigh, knowing she was the canine equivalent of a rebound.

Madchen Two never accompanied us to the beach and rarely posed in any of the family photographs. Once her puppyhood was spent, we more or less lost interest. 'We ought to get a dog,' we'd sometimes say, completely forgetting that we already had one. She came inside to eat, but most of her time was spent out in the pen, slumped in the A-frame doghouse my father had designed and crafted from scrap pieces of redwood.

'Hey,' he'd ask, 'how many dogs can say they live in a redwood house?' This always led to my mother's exhausted 'Oh, Lou, how many dogs can say that they don't live in a goddamned redwood house?'

Throughout the collie and shepherd years, we had a succession of drowsy, secretive cats who seemed to share a unique bond with our mother. 'It's because I open their cans,' she said, though we all knew it ran deeper than that. What they had in common was their claws. That and a deep-seated need to destroy my father's golf bag.

The first cat ran away, and the second was hit by a car. The third passed into a disagreeable old age and died hissing at the kitten who had prematurely arrived to replace her. When, at the age of seven, the fourth cat was diagnosed with feline leukaemia, my mother was devastated.

'I'm going to have Sadie put to sleep,' she said. 'It's for her own good, and I don't want to hear a word about it from any of you. This is hard enough as it is.'

The cat was put down, and then came the anonymous postcards and crank phone calls orchestrated by my sisters and me. The cards announced a miraculous new cure for feline leukaemia, while the callers identified themselves as representatives of Cat Fancy magazine. 'We'd like to use Sadie as our cover story and were hoping to schedule a photo shoot. Can you have her ready by tomorrow?'

We thought a kitten might lift our mother's spirits, but she declined all offers. 'That's it,' she said. 'My cat days are over.'

When Madchen Two developed splenic tumors, our father dropped everything and ran to her side. Evenings were spent at the animal hospital, lying on a mat outside of her cage and adjusting her IV. He'd never afforded her much attention, but her impending death alerted in him a great sense of duty. He was holding her paw when she died, and he spent the next several weeks asking us how many dogs could say they'd lived in a redwood house.

Our mother, in turn, frequently paused beside my father's tattered, urine-stained golf bag and relived memories of her own.

After spending a pet-less year with only one child still living at home, my parents visited a breeder and returned with a Great Dane they named Melina. They loved this dog in proportion to her size, and soon their hearts had no room for anyone else. The house was given over to the dog, rooms redecorated to suit her fancy. Enter your former bedroom and you'd be told, 'You'd better not let Melina catch you in here,' or, 'This is where we come to pee-pee when there's nobody home to let us outside, right, girl?'

The dog was my parents' first true common

interest, and they loved her equally, each in their own way. My mother's love tended toward the horizontal, a pet being little more than a napping companion, something she could look at and say, 'That looks like a good idea. Scoot over, why don't you.' A stranger peeking through the window might think that the two of them had entered a suicide pact. She and the dog sprawled like corpses, their limbs arranged into an eternal embrace. 'God, that felt good,' my mom would say, the two of them waking for a brief stretch. 'Now let's go try it on the living-room floor.'

My father loved the Great Dane for her size, and frequently took her on long, aimless drives during which she'd stick her heavy, anvil-sized head out the window and leak great quantities of foamy saliva. Other drivers pointed and stared, rolling down their windows to shout, 'Hey, you got a saddle for that thing?' When they went out for a walk, there was the inevitable 'Are you walking her, or is it the other way around?'

'Ha, ha,' our father always laughed, as if it were the first time he'd heard it. The attention was addictive, and he enjoyed a pride of accomplishment he'd never felt with any of his children. It was as if he were somehow responsible for her size and stature, as if he'd personally designed her spots and trained her to grow to the size of a pony.

When out with the dog, he carried a leash in one

hand and a shovel in the other. 'Just in case,' he said.

'Just in case what? She dies of a heart attack and you need to bury her?' I didn't get it.

'No,' he'd say. 'It's for her, you know, her . . . business.'

My father was retired, but the dog had business. I was living in Chicago when they first got Melina, and every time I came home, the animal was bigger. Every time there were more Marmaduke cartoons on the refrigerator, and every time my voice grew louder as I asked myself, 'Who are these people?'

'Down, girl,' my parents would chuckle as the dog jumped up, panting for my attention. Her great padded paws reached my waist, then my chest and shoulders, until eventually, her arms wrapped around my neck and her head towering above my own, she came to resemble a dance partner scouting the room for a better offer.

'That's just her way of saying hello,' my mother would say, handing me a towel to wipe off the dog's bubbling seepage. 'Here, you missed a spot on the back of your head.'

Among us children, Melina's diploma from obedience school was seen as the biggest joke since our brother's graduation from Sanderson High School. 'So she's not book smart,' our mother said. 'Big deal. I can fetch my own goddamned newspaper.'

The dog's growth was monitored on a daily basis, and every small accomplishment was captured on film. One could find few pictures of my sister Tiffany, while Melina had entire albums devoted to her terrible twos.

'Hit me,' my mother said on one of my return visits from Chicago. 'No, wait, let me get my camera.' She left the room and returned a few moments later. 'Okay,' she said. 'Now hit me. Better yet, why don't you just pretend to hit me?'

I raised my hand and my mother cried out in pain. 'Ow!' she yelled. 'Somebody help me! This stranger is trying to hurt me, and I don't know why.'

I caught an advancing blur moving in from the left, and the next thing I knew, I was down on the ground, the Great Dane ripping holes in the neck of my sweater. The camera flashed, and my mother roared, 'God, I love that trick.'

I rolled over to protect my face. 'It's not a trick.'

She snapped another picture. 'Oh, don't be so critical. It's close enough.'

With us grown and out of the house, my sisters and I reasonably expected our parents' lives to stand still. Their assignment was to stagnate and live in the past. We were supposed to be the center of their lives, but instead they constructed a new family, consisting of Melina and the founding members of her fan club. Someone who obviously didn't know her too well had given my mother a cheerful stuffed bear with a calico heart stitched onto its chest. According to the manufacturer, the bear's name was

Mumbles, and all it needed in order to thrive was two double-A batteries and a regular diet of hugs.

'Where Mumbles?' my mother would ask, and the dog would jump up and snatch the bear from its hiding place on top of the refrigerator, yanking its body this way and that in hopes of breaking its neck. Occasionally, her teeth would press the on switch and the doomed thing would flail its arms, whispering one of its five messages of goodwill.

'That's my girl,' my mother would say. 'We don't like Mumbles, do we?'

'We?'

During the final years of Madchen Two and the first half of the Melina epoch, I lived with a female cat named Neil who'd been abandoned by a scary alcoholic with long fingernails and a large collection of kimonos. He was a hateful man, and after he moved, the cat was taken in and renamed by my sister Gretchen, who later passed the animal on to me. My mother looked after the cat when I moved from Raleigh, and she flew her to Chicago once I'd found a place and settled in. I'd taken the cheapest apartment I could find, and it showed. Though they were nice, my new neighbors could see no connection between their personal habits and the armies of pests aggressively occupying the building.

Neil caught fourteen mice, and scores of others escaped with missing limbs and tails. In Raleigh, she'd just lain around the house doing nothing, but now she had a real job to do.

Her interests broadened, and she listened intently to the radio, captivated by the political and financial stories that failed to interest me. 'One more word about the Iran-contra hearings and you'll be sleeping next door with the aliens,' I'd say, though we both knew that I didn't really mean it.

Neil was old when she moved to Chicago, and then she got older. The Oliver North testimony now behind her, she started leaving teeth in her bowl and developed the sort of breath that could remove paint. She stopped cleaning herself, and I took to bathing her in the sink. When she was soaking wet, I could see just how thin and brittle she really was. Her kidneys shrank to the size of raisins, and while I wanted what was best for her, I naturally assumed the vet was joking when he suggested dialysis.

In addition to being old, toothless, and incontinent, it seemed that for the cost of a few thousand dollars, she could also spend three days a week hooked up to a machine. 'Sounds awfully tempting,' I said. 'Just give us a few days to think it over.' I took her for a second opinion. Vet number two tested her blood and phoned me a few days later suggesting I consider euthanasia.

I hadn't heard that word since childhood, and immediately recalled a mismatched pair of Japanese schoolboys standing alone in a deserted schoolyard. One of the boys, grossly obese, was attempting to climb the flagpole that towered high above him. Silhouetted against the darkening sky, he hoisted himself a few feet off the ground and clung there, trembling and out of breath. 'I can't do it,' he said. 'This is too hard for me.'

His friend, a gaunt and serious boy named Komatsu, stood below him, offering encouragement. 'Oh, but you can do it. You must,' he said. 'It is required.'

This was a scene I had long forgotten, and thinking of it made me unbearably sad. The boys were characters from Fatty and Skinny, a Japanese movie regularly presented on The CBS Children's Film Festival, a weekly TV series hosted by two puppets and a very patient woman who pretended to laugh at their jokes. My sisters and I watched the program every Saturday afternoon, our gasbag of a collie imposing frequent intermissions.

Having shimmied a few more inches up the pole, Fatty lost his grip and fell down. As he brushed himself off, Skinny ran down the mountain toward the fragile, papery house he shared with his family. This had been Fatty's last chance to prove himself. He'd thought his friend's patience was unlimited, but now he knew that he was wrong. 'Komatsuuuuuuuu!' he yelled. 'Komatsu, please give me one more chance.'

The doctor's voice called me back from the Japanese schoolyard. 'So. The euthanasia,' he said. 'Are you giving it some thought?'

'Yes,' I said. 'As a matter of fact, I am.'

In the end, I returned to the animal hospital and had her put to sleep. When the vet injected the sodium pentobarbital, Neil fluttered her eyes, assumed a nap position, and died. My then-boyfriend stayed to make arrangements, and I ran outside to blubber beside the parked and, unfortunately, locked car. Neil had gotten into the car believing she would live to experience the return trip, and that tore me up. Someone had finally been naive enough to trust me, and I'd rewarded her with death. Racked by guilt, the Youth in Asia sat at their desks and wept bitter tears.

A week after putting her to sleep, I received Neil's ashes in a forest-green can. She'd never expressed any great interest in the outdoors, so I scattered her remains on the carpet and then vacuumed them up. The cat's death struck me as the end of an era. The end of my safe college life, the last of my thirty-inch waist, my faltering relationship with my first real boyfriend – I cried for it all and spent the next several months wondering why so few songs were written about cats.

My mother sent a consoling letter along with a check to cover the cost of the cremation. In the lower-left corner, on the line marked memo, she'd written, 'Pet burning.' I had it coming.

When my mother died and was cremated herself, we worried that, acting on instinct, our father might run out and immediately replace her. Returning from the funeral, my brother, sisters, and I half expected to find Sharon Two standing at the kitchen counter, working the puzzle from TV Guide. 'Sharon One would have gotten five-across,' our father would have scolded. 'Come on, baby, get with it!'

With my mother gone, my father and Melina had each other all to themselves. Though she now occupied the side of the bed left vacant by her former mistress, the dog knew she could never pass as a viable replacement. Her love was too fierce and simple, and she had no talent for argument. Yet she and my father honored their pledge to adore and protect each other. They celebrated anniversaries, regularly renewed their vows, and growled when challenged by outside forces.

'You want me to go where?' When invited to visit one of his children, my father would beg off, saying, 'I can't leave town. Who'd take care of Melina?'

Due to their size, Great Danes generally don't live very long. There are cheeses that last longer. At the age of eleven, gray-bearded and teetering, Melina was a wonder of science. My father massaged her arthritic legs, carried her up the stairs, and lifted her in and out of bed. He treated her the way men in movies treat their ailing wives, the way he might have treated my mother had she allowed such naked displays of helplessness and affection. Melina's era had spanned the final ten years of his married life. The dog had ridden in the family's last station wagon. She'd attended my father's retirement party, lived through my sister's wedding, and celebrated the election of two Republican presidents. She grew weaker and lost her appetite, but against all advice, my father simply could not bear to let go.

The Youth in Asia begged him to end her life.

'I can't do it,' he said. 'This is too hard for me.'

Oh, but you must do it,' said Komatsu. 'It is required.'

A month after Melina was put to sleep, my father returned to the breeder and came home with another Great Dane. A female like Melina, gray spots like Melina, only this one is named Sophie. He tries to love her but readily admits that he may have made a mistake. She's a nice enough dog, but the timing is off.

When walking Sophie through the neighborhood, my father feels not unlike a newly married senior citizen stumbling behind his apathetic young bride. The puppy's stamina embarrasses him, as does her blatant interest in younger men. Passing drivers slow to a stop and roll down their windows. 'Hey,' they yell. 'Are you walking her, or is it the other way around?' Their words remind him of a more gracious era, of milder forces straining against the well-worn leash. He still gets the attention, but now, in response, he just lifts his shovel and continues on his way.

– Let the Lion Dog be Small –

Pekingese dogs were exclusive to the nobility of the
Chinese court. They were considered to be sacred Bud-
dhist spirit-animals born from the mating of lion and
butterfly. Empress Tzu-hsi was devoted to the creatures
and wrote poetically of her 'butterfly lions'. In 1861, during the Opium Wars, a Captain J. Hart Dunn looting
the Summer Palace, took one of Empress Tzu-hsi's dogs,
named her 'Lootie', and gifted her to Queen Victoria, to
live out her days in the royal kennels.

L et the Lion Dog be small;
Let it wear the swelling cape of dignity
    around its neck;
Let it display the billowing standard of pomp in a
    tail held high above its back.
Let its face be black;
Let its forefront be shaggy;
Let its forehead be straight and low, like unto the
    brow of a Boxer.
Let its eyes be large and luminous; let its ears be set
    like the sails of a war-junk;
Let its nose be like the monkey god of the Hindus.
Let its forelegs be bent;
So that it shall not desire to wander far, nor leave

its Imperial home.

Let its body be shaped like a hunting lion, that
    stalks its prey.

Let its feet be tufted with plentiful hair

That its footfall may be soundless,

And for its standard of pomp

Let its tail rival the whisk of a Tibetan yak

Which is flourished to protect the imperial litter
    from flying insects.

For its colour,

Let it be that of a lion – golden sable,
    To be carried in the sleeve of a yellow robe;

Or the colour of a red bear,

Or a black and white bear,

Or striped like a dragon,

So that there may be dogs appropriate to the
    Imperial Wardrobe

And whose fitness to appear at public ceremonies
    shall be judged by their colour and their artistic
    contrast with the Imperial robes.

Let it be lively that it may afford entertainment by
    its gambols;

Let it be timid that it may not involve itself in
    danger;

Let it be domestic in its habits that it may live in
    amity with the other beasts, fishes, or birds that
    find protection in the Imperial Palace.

Let it venerate its ancestors

And deposit offerings in the canine cemetery of the

Forbidden City on each new moon.

Let it be taught to refrain from gadding about;

Let it come to know how to comport itself with the
dignity of a Duchess;

Let it learn to bite the foreign devils instantly.

Let it wash its face like a cat with its paws;

Let it be dainty with its food so that it shall be
known as an Imperial dog by its fastidiousness.

Shark's fins, and curlew's livers and the breasts of
quails,

On these may it be fed;

And for drink give it the tea that is brewed from
the spring buds of the shrub that grows in the
province of Hankow,

Or the milk of the antelopes that pasture in the
Imperial Parks.

Thus shall it preserve its integrity and self-respect;

And for the day of sickness

Let it be anointed with the clarified fat of the leg of
the sacred leopard,

And give it to drink an eggshell from a song thrush

Full of the juice of a custard apple in which has
been dissolved three pinches of shredded
rhinoceros horn,

So shall it remain.

But if it dies, remember thou too art mortal.

French Bulldog

James Thurber

– The Dog that Bit People –

James Thurber (1894–1961) was an American humourist
whose writing and drawings appeared frequently in *The
New Yorker*. He began his career as a newspaperman
and went on to develop an idiosyncratic, observational
humour in hundreds of essays, short stories, fables, and
drawings collected in more than thirty books.

Probably no one man should have as many
dogs in his life as I have had, but there was
more pleasure than distress in them for me except
in the case of an Airedale named Muggs. He gave
me more trouble than all the other fifty-four or
-five put together, although my moment of keenest
embarrassment was the time a Scotch terrier named
Jeannie, who had just had six puppies in the clothes
closet of a fourth floor apartment in New York,
had the unexpected seventh and last at the corner
of Eleventh Street and Fifth Avenue during a walk
she had insisted on taking. Then, too, there was
the prize winning French poodle, a great big black
poodle – none of your little, untroublesome white
miniatures – who got sick riding in the rumble seat

of a car with me on her way to the Greenwich Dog Show. She had a red rubber bib tucked around her throat and, since a rain storm came up when we were halfway through the Bronx, I had to hold over her a small green umbrella, really more of a parasol. The rain beat down fearfully and suddenly the driver of the car drove into a big garage, filled with mechanics. It happened so quickly that I forgot to put the umbrella down and I will always remember, with sickening distress, the look of incredulity mixed with hatred that came over the face of the particular hardened garage man that came over to see what we wanted, when he took a look at me and the poodle. All garage men, and people of that intolerant stripe, hate poodles with their curious hair cut, especially the pom-poms that you got to leave on their hips if you expect the dogs to win a prize.

But the Airedale, as I have said, was the worst of all my dogs. He really wasn't my dog, as a matter of fact: I came home from a vacation one summer to find that my brother Roy had bought him while I was away. A big, burly, choleric dog, he always acted as if he thought I wasn't one of the family. There was a slight advantage in being one of the family, for he didn't bite the family as often as he bit strangers. Still, in the years that we had him he bit everybody but mother, and he made a pass at her once but missed. That was during the month when we suddenly had mice, and Muggs refused to do anything about them. Nobody ever had mice exactly like the mice we had that month. They acted like pet mice, almost like mice somebody had trained. They were so friendly that one night when mother entertained at dinner the Friraliras, a club she and my father had belonged to for twenty years, she put down a lot of little dishes with food in them on the pantry floor so that the mice would be satisfied with that and wouldn't come into the dining room. Muggs stayed out in the pantry with the mice, lying on the floor, growling to himself – not at the mice, but about all the people in the next room that he would have liked to get at. Mother slipped out into the pantry once to see how everything was going. Everything was going fine. It made her so mad to see Muggs lying there, oblivious of the mice – they came running up to her – that she slapped him and he slashed at her, but didn't make it. He was sorry immediately, mother said. He was always sorry, she said, after he bit someone, but we could not understand how she figured this out. He didn't act sorry.

Mother used to send a box of candy every Christmas to the people the Airedale bit. The list finally contained forty or more names. Nobody could understand why we didn't get rid of the dog. I didn't understand it very well myself, but we didn't get rid of him. I think that one or two people tried to poison Muggs – he acted poisoned once in a while – and old Major Moberly fired at him once with his service revolver near the Seneca Hotel in East Broad Street – but Muggs lived to be almost eleven years old and even when he could hardly get around he bit Congressman who had called to see my father on business. My mother had never liked the Congressman – she said the signs of his horoscope showed he couldn't be trusted (he was Saturn with the moon in Virgo) – but she sent him a box of candy that Christmas. He sent it right back, probably because he suspected it was trick candy. Mother persuaded herself it was all for the best that the dog had bitten him, even though father lost an important business association because of it. 'I wouldn't be associated with such a man,' mother said, 'Muggs could read him like a book.'

We used to take turns feeding Muggs to be on his good side, but that didn't always work. He was never in a very good humor, even after a meal. Nobody knew exactly what was the matter with him, but whatever it was it made him irascible, especially in the mornings. Roy never felt very well in the morning, either, especially before breakfast, and once when he came downstairs and found that Muggs had moodily chewed up the morning paper he hit him in the face with a grapefruit and then jumped up on the dining room table, scattering dishes and silverware and spilling the coffee. Muggs' first free leap carried him all the way across the table and into a brass fire screen in front of the gas grate but he was back on his feet in a moment and in the end he got Roy and gave him a pretty vicious bite in the leg. Then he was all over it; he never bit anyone more than once at a time. Mother always mentioned that as an argument in his favor; she said he had a quick temper but that he didn't hold a grudge. She was forever defending him. I think she liked him because he wasn't well. 'He's not strong,' she would say, pityingly, but that was inaccurate; he may not have been well but he was terribly strong.

One time my mother went to the Chittenden Hotel to call on a woman mental healer who was lecturing in Columbus on the subject of 'Harmonious Vibrations'. She wanted to find out if it was possible to get harmonious vibrations into a dog. 'He's a large tan-colored Airedale,' mother explained. The woman said that she had never treated a dog but she advised my mother to hold the thought that he did not bite and would not bite. Mother was holding the thought the very next morning when Muggs got the iceman but she blamed that slip-up on the iceman. 'If you didn't think he would bite you, he wouldn't,' mother told him. He stomped out of the house in a terrible jangle of vibrations.

One morning when Muggs bit me slightly, more or less in passing, I reached down and grabbed his short stumpy tail and hoisted him into the air. It was a foolhardy thing to do and the last time I saw my mother, about six months ago, she said she didn't know what possessed me. I don't either, except that I was pretty mad. As long as I held the dog off the floor by his tail he couldn't get at me, but he twisted and jerked so, snarling all the time, that I realized I couldn't hold him that way very long. I carried him to the kitchen and flung him onto the floor and shut the door on him just as he crashed against it. But I forgot about the backstairs. Muggs went up the backstairs and down the front stairs and had me cornered in the living room. I managed to get up onto the mantelpiece above the fireplace, but it gave way and came down with a tremendous crash throwing a large marble clock, several vases, and myself heavily to the floor. Muggs was so alarmed by the racket that when I picked myself up he had disappeared. We couldn't find him anywhere, although we whistled and shouted, until old Mrs. Detweiler called after dinner that night. Muggs had bitten her once, in the leg, and she came into the living room only after we assured her that Muggs had run away. She had just seated herself when, with a great growling and scratching of claws, Muggs emerged from under a davenport where he had been quietly hiding all the time, and bit her again. Mother examined the bite and put arnica on it and told Mrs. Detweiler that it was only a bruise. 'He just bumped you,' she said. But Mrs. Detweiler left the house in a nasty state of mind.

Lots of people reported our Airedale to the

police but my father held a municipal office at the time and was on friendly terms with the police. Even so, the cops had been out a couple of times – once when Muggs bit Mrs. Rufus Sturtevant and again when he bit Lieutenant-Governor Malloy – but mother told them that it hadn't been Muggs' fault but the fault of the people who were bitten. 'When he starts for them, they scream,' she explained, 'and that excites him.' The cops suggested that it might be a good idea to tie the dog up, but mother said that it mortified him to be tied up and that he wouldn't eat when he was tied up.

Muggs at his meals was an unusual sight. Because of the fact that if you reached toward the floor he would bite you, we usually put his food plate on top of an old kitchen table with a bench alongside the table. Muggs would stand on the bench and eat. I remember that my mother's Uncle Horatio, who boasted that he was the third man up Missionary Ridge, was splutteringly indignant when he found out that we fed the dog on a table because we were afraid to put his plate on the floor. He said he wasn't afraid of any dog that ever lived and that he would put the dog's plate on the floor if we would give it to him. Roy said that if Uncle Horatio had fed Muggs on the ground just before the battle he would have been the first man up Missionary Ridge. Uncle Horatio was furious. 'Bring him in! Bring him in now!' he shouted. 'I'll feed the – on the floor!' Roy was all for giving him a chance, but my father wouldn't hear of it. He said that Muggs had already been fed. 'I'll feed him again!' bawled Uncle Horatio. We had quite a time quieting him.

In his last year Muggs used to spend practically all of his time outdoors. He didn't like to stay in the house for some reason or other – perhaps it held too many unpleasant memories for him. Anyway, it was hard to get him to come in and as a result the garbage man, the iceman, and the laundryman wouldn't come near the house. We had to haul the garbage down to the corner, take the laundry out and bring it back, and meet the iceman a block from home. After this had gone on for some time we hit on an ingenious arrangement for getting the dog in the house so that we could lock him up while the gas meter was read, and so on. Muggs was afraid of only one thing, an electrical storm. Thunder and lightning frightened him out of his senses (I think he thought a storm had broken the day the mantel-piece fell). He would rush into the house and hide under a bed or in a clothes closet. So we fixed up a thunder machine out of a long narrow piece of sheet iron with a wooden handle on one end. Mother would shake this vigorously when she wanted to get Muggs into the house. It made an excellent imitation of thunder, but I suppose it was the most roundabout system for running a household that was ever devised. It took a lot out of mother.

A few months before Muggs died, he got to 'seeing things'. He would rise slowly from the floor, growling low, and stalk stiff-legged and menacing toward nothing at all. Sometimes the Thing would be just a little to the right or left of a visitor. Once a Fuller Brush salesman got hysterics. Muggs came wandering into the room like Hamlet' following his father's ghost. His·eyes were fixed on a spot just to the left of the Fuller Brush man, who stood it until Muggs was about three slow, creeping paces from him. Then he shouted. Muggs wavered on past him into the hallway grumbling to himself but the Fuller man went on shouting. I think mother had to throw a pan of cold water on him before he stopped. That was the way she used to stop us boys when we got into fights.

Muggs died quite suddenly one night. Mother wanted to bury him in the family lot under a marble stone with some such inscription as 'Flights of angels sing thee to thy rest' but we persuaded her it was against the law. In the end we just put up a smooth board above his grave along a lonely road. On the board I wrote with an indelible pencil 'Cave Canem'. Mother was quite pleased with the simple classic dignity of the old Latin epitaph.

Heli Chatelain

– Dog and Jackal –

Heli Chatelain (1859–1908), was a brilliant Swiss linguist, and passionate advocate for the abolition of slavery. In 1885 he travelled to Angola's capital Luanda to study Kimbundu and record oral histories in both Kimbundu and English. The stories he recorded touch universal themes and questions, such as why the dog chose life with humans over life in the wild. This story of Dog and Jackal appears in Chatelain's *Folk Tales of Angola*.

Jackal used to be in the bush with his kinsman, Dog. Jackal then sends Dog saying, 'Go to the houses to fetch some fire. When thou comest with it, we will burn the prairie of grass; so as to catch the locusts and eat.' Dog agreed.

He started: arrived at the village. He enters a house; finds a woman, who is feeding her child with mush. Dog sat down; fire, he will not take it. The woman has fed her child; she scrapes the pot. She takes mush; she gives it to Dog. Dog eats; thinks, saying 'Why I am all the time just dying of hunger in the bush; in the village there is good eating.' The Dog settled there.

Jackal behind where he stayed, looked for the other, who was sent for fire; he does not appear.

The Jackal whenever he is howling, people say 'The Jackal is howling, tway.' But no; he is speaking, saying: 'I am surprised, I, Jackal of Ngonga; Dog, whom I sent for fire, when he found mush, he was seduced; he stayed for good.'

Roald Amundsen

– *from* The South Pole: An Account of the Norwegian Antarctic Expedition in the 'Fram', 1910–1912 –

Norwegian polar explorer Amundsen (1872–1928), and a team of five men and fifty-two dogs left their base camp for the South Pole on 19 October 1911, reaching the Pole on 14 December, a month before Captain Scott's ill-fated expedition. Amundsen credited the success of his mission to his dogs, and his team's skilled handling of them. The men arrived safely back at base camp on 25 January 1912, with eleven surviving dogs.

B efore I proceed to our further equipment, I must say a few more words about the dogs. The greatest difference between Scott's and my equipment lay undoubtedly in our choice of draught animals. We had heard that Scott, relying on his own experience, and that of Shackleton, had come to the conclusion that Manchurian ponies were superior to dogs on the Barrier. Among those who were acquainted with the Eskimo dog, I do not suppose I was the only one who was startled on first hearing this. Afterwards, as I read the different narratives and was able to form an accurate opinion of the conditions of surface and going, my astonishment became even greater. Although I had never seen this part of the Antarctic regions, I was not long in forming an opinion diametrically opposed to that of Shackleton and Scott, for the conditions both of going and surface were precisely what one would desire for sledging with Eskimo dogs, to judge from the descriptions of these explorers. If Peary could make a record trip on the Arctic ice with dogs, one ought, surely, with equally good tackle, to be able to beat Peary's record on the splendidly even surface of the Barrier. There must be some misunderstanding or other at the bottom of the Englishmen's estimate of the Eskimo dog's utility in the Polar regions. Can it be that the dog has not understood his master? Or is it the master who has not understood his dog? The right footing must be established from the out-set; the dog must understand that he has to obey in everything, and the master must know how to make himself respected. If obedience is once established, I am convinced that the dog will be superior to all other draught animals over these long distances.

Another very important reason for using the dog is that this small creature can much more easily cross the numerous slight snow-bridges that are not to be avoided on the Barrier and on the glaciers. If a dog falls into a crevasse, there is no great harm done; a tug at his harness and he is out again; but it is another matter with a pony. This comparatively large and heavy animal of course falls through far more easily, and if this happens, it is a long and stiff job to get the beast hauled up again – unless, indeed, the traces have broken and the pony lies at the bottom of a crevasse 1,000 feet deep.

And then there is the obvious advantage that dog can be fed on dog. One can reduce one's pack little by little, slaughtering the feebler ones and feeding the chosen with them. In this way they get fresh meat. Our dogs lived on dog's flesh and pemmican the whole way, and this enabled them to do splendid work.

And if we ourselves wanted a piece of fresh meat we could cut off a delicate little fillet; it tasted to us as good as the best beef. The dogs do not object at all; as long as they get their share they do not mind what part of their comrade's carcass it comes from. All that was left after one of these canine meals was the teeth of the victim – and if it had been a really hard day, these also disappeared.

If we take a step farther, from the Barrier to the plateau, it would seem that every doubt of the dog's superiority must disappear. Not only can one get the dogs up over the huge glaciers that lead to the plateau, but one can make full use of them the whole way. Ponies, on the other hand, have to be left at the foot of the glacier, while the men themselves have the doubtful pleasure of acting as ponies. As I understand Shackleton's account, there can be no question of hauling the ponies over the steep and crevassed glaciers. It must be rather hard to have to abandon one's motive power voluntarily when only a quarter of the distance has been covered. I for my part prefer to use it all the way.

From the very beginning I saw that the first part of our expedition, from Norway to the Barrier, would be the most dangerous section. If we could only reach the Barrier with our dogs safe and well, the future would be bright enough. Fortunately, all my comrades took the same view of the matter, and with their cooperation we succeeded not only in bringing the dogs safely to our field of operations, but in landing them in far better condition than when we received them. Their number was also considerably increased on the way, which seems to be another proof of a flourishing state of things. To protect them against damp and heat we laid a loose deck of planed boards about 3 inches above the fixed deck, an arrangement by which all the rain and spray ran underneath the dogs. In this way we kept them out of the water, which must always be running from side to side on the deck of a deep-laden vessel on her way to the Antarctic Ocean. Going through the tropics this loose deck did double service. It always afforded a somewhat cool surface, as there was a fresh current of air between the two decks. The main deck, which was black with tar, would have been unbearably hot for the animals; the false deck was high, and kept fairly white during the whole voyage. We carried awnings in addition, chiefly on account of the dogs. These awnings could be stretched over the whole vessel and give the dogs constant protection from the burning sun.

I still cannot help smiling when I think of the compassionate voices that were raised here and there – and even made their way into print – about the 'cruelty to animals' on board the Fram. Presumably these cries came from tender-hearted individuals who themselves kept watch-dogs tied up.

Translated by A. G. Chater

– Psychogeography:
Going to the Dogs –

Will Self is a prodigious British novelist and political commentator. Self has a Jack Russell Terrier, a strain of hunting dog bred to flush out foxes which are in plentiful supply in his London neighbourhood.

Crumbling the progesterone into Cyril's Pedigree Chum worked, and a litter of Jack Russell puppies duly arrived. Staying with Cyril's human 'owners' in the Vale of Pershore, my ten-year-old got up early and spent the morning with the little bundles of joy. He battened on to the spunkiest one of the litter, a bite-sized doglet he dubbed Maglorian. Why Maglorian? Well, the child has a considerable – and in my view, misplaced – affection for the works of J. K. Rowling, and apparently there's a centaur called Magorian that lives in the Magic Forest adjacent to Hogwarts. However, Magorian, he explained, 'sounds too gory', so the 'L' was inserted so that 'he can be "Glory" for short'.

But I wasn't willing to call anything Glory for short – it's either too homoerotic, or too patriotic; reminiscent either of the glory holes of Manhattan's Mineshaft in the early Eighties, or else of 'Land of

Hope and Glory'; either way, you won't get me wandering round South London parks shouting 'Glory!' at the top of my voice – what do you think I am, a cabinet minister?

Disputes about nomenclature set to one side there was no further let or hindrance to the beast pitching up, which, a few weeks later he did. Now, my resistance to canine culture is a matter of record: not for me the shit-picking, dull-walking two-step of the tethered promenade, nor the exorbitant veterinary bills; to round up sheep with a beautifully trained collie, using only a whistle and a crook is one thing, but to lower your emotional horizon to the level of these urban pavement-crawlers, selectively bred to fulfil the furry baby fantasies of the frustrated and the barren, well, that suckles.

Still, it was pointed out to me, quite forcibly, that small boys need dogs, and so there was Maglorian: an itty-bitty fait accompli with tan and cream markings. Then, horror of horrors, a dreadful thing happened, the Dog Instigator had to go away for a few days leaving me in sole charge of the puppy. Well, I may be a hard-hearted bastard, but I'm not a robot, and an infant is an infant, even one with a muzzle and claws. What I'm scratching at here is that – in psychoanalytic jargon – Maglorian and I both cathected. Of course, he has imprinted me radically differently to the way I have him: to him I am a noble pack leader, scouring the horizon for the next kill, and planning how to separate the vulnerable strag-gler from the herd, then rip its throat out; whereas, to me, Maglorian's an itty-bitty . . . well, I think I'll spare you any further nausea.

My dog ownership is gifting me some new insights into the patch of town I've been pissing in for the past decade; there's an entire stratum of local society that I've previously been excluded from: the nervy lady who looks like the late Dick Emery doing a drag act, and who punctually at 9.00 am walks her miniature spaniel along our road; the muscular six-foot clone in the bomber jacket with the short-haired Alsatian; the elderly gent who has come, inexorably, to resemble his arthritic Airedale terrier – with all of them I am now on nodding terms. Actually, I've always been on nodding terms with them, but now the nod is just a fraction deeper, the chin tucked down to the chest in a submissive way as we mutu-ally acknowledge the Suzerainty of the Hound.

No, it's not the local dog people that bother me, it's the ignorant masses who coo and bill over Maglo-rian wherever I take him. I swear, if another femme d'un certain age, or broody couple, comes waggling up to me, speaking in baby talk, and twittering away about how sweeeet he is, I'm going to puke. Have these people no shame? Of course, I understand that they don't really want to have dog babies any more than I do, it's just an atavistic impulse, of the same order that makes perfectly respectable stockbrokers put on three-piece tweed suits and shoot more pheasants than they could ever possibly eat.

Perversely, although we chose Maglorian on the grounds that a small dog was better for town, the Dog Instigator has been reading up on Jack Russells, and it turns out that they are regarded as 'big dogs wearing little dog suits'. I thought as much, when the five-month-old pup happily trotted along behind me for a strenuous six-mile walk. This is no lapdog to be concealed in a feminine muff (or ruff, if you're prudish), but a noble fox terrier, a working dog, capable of tearing Vulpes vulpes apart in seconds. Good thing too – since there are plenty of foxes in this neck of the woods.

Yes, as soon as Maglorian is full grown I'm going to take him out into the Magic Forest and let him bring his near-namesake to bay. A horse with a man growing out of its back? Goddamn mutants shouldn't be allowed.

Roger Scruton

– *from* Loving Animals –

Sir Roger Scruton is a philosopher, public commentator, essayist, and author of over forty books on philosophy, aesthetics and politics. He engages in contemporary political and cultural debates from the standpoint of a conservative thinker. He is a fellow of the Royal Society of Literature and the British Academy.

Each species is different, and when it comes to dogs there is no doubt, not only that dogs reciprocate the affection of their masters, but also that they become attached to their masters as individuals, in a way that renders their masters irreplaceable in their affections, so much so that the grief of a dog may strike us as desolate beyond anything else that we, who have access even in extremity to consolation, could really feel. The focussed devotion of a dog is – when it occurs (and not all dogs are capable of it) – one of the most moving of all the gifts that we receive from animals, all the more moving for not being truly a gift, but a need. It seems to me that the recipient of such a love is under a duty to the creature that offers it, and that this creates a quite special ground for love that we must take into account. The owner of a loving dog has a duty of care beyond that of the owner of a horse. To neglect or abandon such a dog is to betray a trust that creates an objective obligation towards an individual. Hence my neighbour is right to think that her obligation to her dog takes precedence over any duty to care for the wildlife whose welfare he is compromising. She occupies one pole of a relation of trust, and it would be a moral deficiency in her to assume the right to enjoy her dog's unswerving affection while denying him what she can easily provide by way of a reward for it. Hence I don't judge her adversely for her irritating dog or her equally irritating love of it: the fault is mine, like the fault of being upset by the selfishness of families, as they strive to secure the best seats on a train. Each of us has a sphere of love, and he is bound to the others who inhabit it.

That said, however, we should still make a distinction between the right way and the wrong way to love a dog. Dogs are individuals, in the way that all animals are individuals. But they have, if it can be so expressed, a higher degree of individuality than birds, certainly a higher degree of individuality than insects. By this I mean that their wellbeing is more bound up with their affections and their character, than is the wellbeing of members of other species. A bird relates to its surroundings as a member of its species, but not as one who created for itself an individual network of expectations and fears.

The loving dog is dependent on individual people, and knows that he is so dependent. He responds to his surroundings in ways that distinguish individuals within it, and recognises demands that are addressed specifically to him, and to which he must respond. His emotions, simple though they are, are learned responses, which bear the imprint of a history of mutual dealings.

[. . .] Now it seems to me that the right way to love a dog is to love him not as a person, but as a creature that has been raised to the edge of personhood, so as to look into a place that is opaque to him but from which emerge signals that he understands in another way than we who send them. If we base our love for our dog on the premise that he, like us, is a person, then we damage both him and ourselves. We damage him by making demands that no animal may fully understand – holding him to account in ways that make no sense to him. We will feel bound to keep him alive, as we keep each other alive, for the sake of a relation that being personal, is also eternal. It seems to me that a person loves his dog wrongly when he does not have him put down when the decay is irreversible. But it is not so much the damage done to the dog that matters: it is the damage done to the person. The love of a dog is in an important sense cost-free. The greatest criminal can enjoy it. No dog demands virtue or honour of his master, and all dogs will leap to their master's defence, even when it is the forces of good that are coming to arrest him. Dogs do not judge, and their love is unconditional only because it has no conception of conditions. From a dog, therefore, we can enjoy the kind of endorsement that requires no moral labour to earn it. And this is what we see around us: the dwindling of human affection, which is always conditional and always dependent on moral work, and its replacement by the cost-free love of pets.

Such a love wants to have it both ways: to preserve the pre-lapsarian innocence of its object, while believing the object capable nevertheless of moral judgement. The dog is a dumb animal; but for that very reason he is seen as right in all his judgements, bestowing his affection on worthy objects, and endorsing his master through his love. This is the root cause of the sentimentalisation of animal life that makes a film like Bambi so poisonous – leading people to 'dollify' animals, while believing the animals to be 'in the right' and always endowed with the moral advantage. But you cannot have it both ways: either animals are outside the sphere of moral judgement, or they are not. If they are outside it, then their behaviour cannot be taken as proof of their 'innocence'. If they are inside it, then they may sometimes be guilty and deserving of blame.

Human love is of many kinds. In its highest form, it comes as a gift, freely bestowed on another person along with the offer of support. But such love does not come without cost. There is a cost to the subject, and to the object. Love can be betrayed by its object, when he shows himself to be unworthy to receive it, and incapable of returning it. And to undergo this experience is one of the greatest of human griefs. But love for that very reason imposes a cost on its object, who must live up to the trust bestowed on him, and do his best to deserve it. Love is a moral challenge that we do not always meet, and in the effort to meet it we study to improve ourselves and to live as we should. It is for this reason that we are suspicious of loveless people – people who do not offer love and who therefore, in the normal run of things, do not receive it. It is not simply that they are outside the fold of human affection. It is that they are cut off from the principal spur to human goodness, which is the desire to live up to the demands of a person who matters to them more than they matter to themselves.

Clearly, if we conceive human love in that way, we can see that we all have a strong motive to avoid it: we do not benefit by avoiding it, and it is always a mistake to try, as we know from the tragedy of *King Lear*. Nevertheless, life is simpler without inter-personal love, since it can be lived at a lower level, beneath the glare of moral judgement. And that is the *bad* reason for lavishing too much feeling on a pet. Devoted animals provide an escape-route from human affection, and so make that affection super-fluous. Of course, people can find themselves so beaten down by life, so deprived of human love, that through no fault of their own, they devote them-selves to the care of an animal, by way of keeping the lamp of affection alive. Such is Flaubert's *Coeur Simple*, whose devotion to her parrot was in no way a moral failing. But that kind of devotion, which is the residue of genuine moral feeling, is a virtue in the one who displays it, and has little in common with the Bambyism that is now growing all around us, and which seeks to rewrite our relations with other animals in the language of rights.

I have argued against the ideas of animal rights elsewhere. My argument stems, not from a disrespect for animals, but from a respect for moral reasoning, and for the concepts – right, duty, obligation, virtue – which it employs and which depend at every point on the distinctive features of self-conciousness. But perhaps the greatest damage done by the idea of animal rights is the damage to animals themselves. Elevated in this way to the plane of moral conscious-ness, they find themselves unable to respond to the distinctions that morality requires. They do not distinguish right from wrong; they cannot recog-nise the call of duty or the binding obligations of the moral law. And because of this we judge them purely in terms of their ability to share our domes-tic ambience, to profit from our affection, and from time to time to reciprocate it in their own mute and dependent way. And it is precisely this that engenders our unscrupulous favouritism – the favouritism that has made it a crime in my country to shoot a cat, however destructive its behaviour, but a praiseworthy action to poison a mouse, and thereby to infect the food-chain on which so many animals depend.

It is not that we should withdraw our love from our favourite animals: to the extent that they depend on that love to that extent we should continue to provide it. But we must recognise that by loving them as individuals we threaten the animals who cannot easily be loved in any such way. Loving our dogs and cats we put strain upon the natural order that is felt most grievously by the birds and the beasts of the field. And even if those creatures have no rights, this does not cancel the fact that we have duties towards them – duties that become every day more serious and demanding, as we humans expand to take over the habitat that we confiscate without scruple and enjoy without remorse. And our lack of scruple is only amplified by the sentimental attitudes that are nurtured by the love of pets, and which inculcate in us the desire for easy-going, cost-free and self-congratulatory affections, and which thereby undermine the human virtue on which the rest of nature most depends.

Lurcher

Mikhail Bulgakov

– *from* The Heart of a Dog –

Russian novelist and playwright Mikhail Bulgakov
(1891–1940) qualified as a doctor, but gave up medicine
to become a writer. His satirical books were critical of
Soviet Russia, and he was prohibited from publishing.
The Master and Margarita, his most celebrated work, was
published thirty years after his death, and features Ace
of Diamonds, a 'sharp-eared, muscular, ash-coloured
dog with extremely intelligent eyes'. *Heart of a Dog*, written in 1929, is a parable of the Russian Revolution.

There is absolutely no call to learn to read when
one can smell meat a mile off. Nevertheless,
if you happen to live in Moscow and you have any
brains at all, you are bound to pick up your letters,
even without any particular instruction. Of the forty
thousand dogs in Moscow there can only be the odd
idiot who doesn't know the letters for 'salami'.

Sharik had begun to learn by colours. When
he was only just four months old they hung out
blue-green signs all over Moscow bearing the legend MSPO – the meat trade. As we said before, all
that was quite unnecessary because you can smell
meat anyway. It even led to some confusion when
Sharik, whose sense of smell had been disorientated

by the stink of petrol from a passing car, took his cue from the caustic blue-green colour and made a raid on Golubizner Bros, electric goods shop. There at the brothers' shop the dog made the acquaintance of isolated electric cable, something to be reckoned with even more seriously than a cabby's horse-whip. That occasion should be considered the beginning of Sharik's education. Already out on the pavement it occurred to Sharik that 'blue' did not necessarily mean 'meat' and, tail tucked between his legs, he recalled, howling from the burning pain, that at all butchers' signs the first letter on the left was a golden or reddish curlicue shaped something like a sleigh.

As time went on he improved his knowledge still more. 'A' he learned from the legend 'Glavryba' on the corner of Mokhovaya Street and, after that, from the same source, 'B' – it was easier for him to sneak up from the tail of the word ryba (fish) because there was a militiaman on duty at its head.

Square tiles on the corners of houses in Moscow always, unfailingly meant 'Cheese'. The black samovar-tap at the head of the next word stood for the ex-owner of a chain of cheese shops whose name was Chichkin, for mountains of red Dutch cheese and ferocious shop assistants, the brutes, dog-haters to a man, and sawdust on the floor and that repulsive, evil smelling cheese . . .

If there was someone playing the harmonica,

which was really not much better than Beloved Aida, and at the same time there was a smell of sausages, then the first letters on the white hoardings could be comfortably deciphered as 'impro' which meant 'improper language and tipping are strictly forbidden'. In such places fights would suddenly boil up like whirlpools and people would hit each other in the face with their fists, though to be honest this did not happen often, whereas dogs were always catching it either from napkins or boots.

If slightly off hams or tangerines were on show in the window, the letters read gr-gr-ro-ocers. If there were dark bottles with a nasty liquid content . . . Wer-wi-ner-er-wine . . . Eliseyev Bros., ex-owners.

The unknown gentleman who had enticed the dog to the door of his luxurious first floor flat rang the bell, and the dog immediately raised his eyes to the large black card with gold lettering hanging to one side of the wide door panelled with rosy, ribbed glass. The first three letters he made out straightaway: 'P-r-o – Pro'. But after that came a paunchy two-sided trashy sort of a letter which might mean anything: surely not 'Pro-letariat'? thought Sharik with surprise...

'Impossible!' He raised his nose, took another sniff at the fur coat and thought with conviction: 'No, not so much as a whiff of the proletariat. A learned word and God knows what it means.'

Unexpectedly, a cheerful light came on behind

the pink glass, showing up the black card even more vividly. The door opened without a sound and a pretty young woman in a white apron and a lace cap materialised before the dog and his master. The former was conscious of a divine wave of warmth and from the woman's skirt there wafted a scent like lily-of-the-valley.

This is life, thought the dog, I really fancy this.

'Do us the honour, Mister Sharik,' The gentleman ironically ushered him over the threshold, and Sharik reverently did him the honour, wagging his tail.

The rich entrance hall was full of things. A full-length mirror impressed itself on the dog's memory with an immediate reflection of a second shaggy, ragged Sharik. There were a terrifying pair of antlers high up on the wall, endless fur coats and galoshes and an opalescent tulip with electricity hanging from the ceiling.

'Where did you find such a creature, Philip Philipovich?' asked the woman, smiling and helping him take off the heavy coat with its silver-fox lining. 'Good heavens! He's covered in mange!'

'Nonsense. Where do you see mange?' demanded the gentleman with abrupt severity.

Having taken off his coat he turned out to be dressed in a black suit of English cloth and a golden chain glinted joyfully but not too brightly across his stomach.

'Wait now, don't wiggle, phew . . . don't wiggle, stupid. Hm! That's not mange . . . stand still, you devil! Hm! Aha. It's a burn. What villain scalded you, eh? Stand still, will you?'

'That jail-bird of a chef, the chef!' the dog pronounced with pathetic eyes and whimpered.

'Zina,' the gentleman ordered. 'Into the consulting room with him this instant and bring me my smock.'

The woman whistled and snapped her fingers and, after a moment's doubt, the dog followed her. Together they proceeded along a narrow, dimly-lit corridor, passed one varnished door, went on to the end and then turned left into a dark cupboard of a room to which the dog took an instant dislike because of the ominous smell. The darkness clicked and was transformed into blinding day; sparkling, shining white lights beaming in at him from every side.

Oh no, you don't, the dog howled inwardly. Thanks very much, but I'm not putting up with this. Now I understand, may the devil take you and your salami. You've brought me to a dog's hospital and now you'll pour castor oil down me and chop up that flank of mine which is too sore to be touched with your knives!

'Hey, where are you off to?' cried the woman called Zina.

The dog twisted away from her, gathered

himself together and suddenly struck the door with his good side so violently that the thud could be heard all over the flat. He rebounded and began to spin round and round on the spot like a whipped top, overturning a white basket with chunks of cotton wool. As he spun the walls revolved around him with their glass cupboards full of shiny instruments and he kept getting glimpses of a white apron and a distorted woman's face.

'Where are you going, you shaggy devil?' yelled Zina in desperation. 'You hellhound, you!'

Where's the back stairs? wondered the dog. He rolled himself up into a ball and dashed himself against the glass in the hope that this might be a second door. A cloud of splinters flew out, clattering and tinkling, a fat jar leapt out at him full of nasty red stuff which immediately spilt all over the floor, stinking. The real door opened.

'Stop, you b-brute!' shouted the gentleman struggling into his smock which was half on, half off and seizing the dog by the leg. 'Zina, get him by the scruff, the blighter.'

'H-heavens alive, what a dog!'

The door opened wider still and in burst another person of male gender in a smock. Crushing the broken glass underfoot, he made a dive not for the dog but for the cupboard, opened it, and immediately the room was filled with a sweet, sickly smell. Then this person flung himself on the dog from above,

126

stomach first, and Sharik enthusiastically sunk his teeth into his leg just above the shoelaces. The person grunted but did not lose his head. The sickly liquid set the dog gasping for breath, his head spun and his legs gave way and he keeled over sideways. Thank you, it's the end of my troubles, he thought dreamily as he collapsed onto sharp fragments of glass. This is it. Farewell, Moscow! I'll never see Chichkin again, nor the proletarians, nor Cracow salami. I'm on my way to heaven for the dog's life I bore with such patience. Brothers, murderers, why did you do this to me?

And with that he finally keeled over on his side and breathed his last.

When life returned, his head was still spinning gently, he felt slightly sick and it was as though he had no sore side, it had sunk into sweet oblivion. The dog opened a sleepy right eye and out of the corner of it perceived that he was tightly bandaged round the side and stomach.

So they did me after all, the sons of bitches, he thought vaguely. But they made a good job of it, I'll say that for them.

Brigitte Bardot

– Open Letter –

Brigitte Bardot established the Fondation Brigitte Bardot in 1987. With the Dalai-Lama as a Membre d'honneur, the FBB runs three animal sanctuaries in France. Mme Bardot passionately campaigns and educates on the ethical treatment of all animals, although she has said 'my favourite animals are dogs'.

There are too many dogs! Sometimes the truth hurts, but that *is* the truth.

The cost of this canine population explosion is a cycle of abandonment, overcrowded animal refuges and euthanasia.

At the Mare Auzou, in the Eure et Loire, one of my Foundation's three animal rescue centres, we have almost two hundred dogs whose desperation fills me with sadness, because, though Mare Auzou is a wonderful place, all these animals want and need is the warmth and kindness of an owner and a home.

At our shelters there are pedigree dogs, casually purchased at astronomical prices and then cast aside: Huskies, Labradors, Poodles, Bichon Frises, German Shepherds, all of which we have sterilised, tattooed and vaccinated ready for a new home. We have adorable crossbreeds and mongrels: cute, intelligent, cheeky or mournful, dog or bitch, of all shapes and sizes, and all they want is to make a new owner happy!

It's criminal to breed from your pet and sell puppies through the small ads because those puppies soon grow, and with them grows the number of abandoned dogs fated to be put down in overflowing animal refuges.

And buying puppies, often ill and of doubtful origins, for their weight in gold from pet shops and animal supermarkets which pop up like mushrooms, selling anything to anyone, sustains an illicit trade from Eastern Europe; an unremitting, deadly, money-making cycle without a thought for the canine victims.

Today, thousands of dogs will arrive in animal refuges all over France, with uncertain futures and only two possible outcomes: adoption or fatal injection! And most animal refuges are desperately short of funds.

Let's face the facts, stop burying our heads in the sand. Imports and exports of dogs must stop, quotas must be imposed on breeders, people should be prevented from breeding their pets, and above all sterilise bitches. Stop the idea that it would be nice if the adorable little dog who we love so much could only have some babies of her own! A litter of puppies, or kittens is so cute, yes! but what does the future hold for those little ones, and for the generations that follow?

The most precious and beautiful demonstration of the love we have for our pets, is to do what we can to reduce this relentless population growth. Doing so will prevent distressed animals being cast into refuges, and prevent torture and euthanasia. Sterilising a cat or dog is not unnatural and is not bad for their health. In fact in bitches sterilisation extends life expectancy by reducing the risk of breast cancer. Check with your vet. Because by stopping your own pet from reproducing, you massively increase the chances of adoption for all those other dogs waiting hopefully in over populated refuges and dogs' homes.

Loving, feeding, caring for, but not sterilising your pet, condemns more animals than you could imagine. Please: think first.

A. A. Gill

– Why Dogs Are Still a Man's Best Friend –

A. A. Gill (1954–2016) was a British journalist, travel writer, and television and restaurant critic. He wrote humorous articles for *The Sunday Times*, *Vanity Fair*, *Esquire* and *GQ*. These were filed by phone due to his profound dyslexia. In 2004 he refused to file copy for a commission with *Esquire* unless he received a Parson Russell Terrier Puppy. His editor took him at his word and the dog was duly delivered to his London home.

I'm looking at a bunch of flowers. It's expensive, hand-plaited and knotted, £70 minimum. They're for me. I've been bunched. Someone wanted to say it with flowers. The note that came with them says, 'Sorry' but the flowers say, 'You're a fucking monster.' They say it in a cappella, colour-coordinated, greenly scented harmony.

They're from a man. When men send each other flowers it means one of four things. It means one of them is a gardener, one of them is an interior decorator or cheating on an interior decorator, one of them is dead, or one of them is a monster. The man who sent them to me was an editor, so none of the above. I checked my pulse and it must be me: I'm either the interior decorator or the monster. I have become a diva, the Pavarotti of print. I'm toying with the idea of insisting on my own personal sub-editor. I want Mario to do my picture and Nicky my hair. I want my name above the headline. I want my name to be the headline. I want my prose in bold. I want editorial control of readers' letters. I want control of readers. I want, I want . . . How did it end up like this? How did I get bunched by an editor? Because I'd behaved like Lady Victoria Hervey at a TV soap opera awards party. My Great Aunt Netta used to say, 'If it's a choice between being brilliant and being nice, be nice. And if you don't have the choice (and you don't) be nice, because you don't have to be brilliant to be nice.' I know what kicked all this off, when my inner monster came out of the closet. It was the dog. An editor (not the floral one, another one) called to inquire politely, nicely, about a piece I owed. It was late, exceedingly late, later than a Bulgarian tackle, later than the USA joining a world war, later than Jools Holland and David Letterman, so late, in fact, that the entire magazine was waiting on the printers' slipway, so did I think perhaps I might let them have it?

Instead of saying sorry, which would have been the Aunt Netta, nice option, I said, 'I'll give you the piece by Friday, if you give me a puppy on Monday.' And instead of saying, 'Fuck off, you megalomaniac little madam', which would have been the normal sane reaction, the editor waited a beat and said, 'What breed?' And then instead of me saying, 'Ho, ho, ho, I was only joking', I stepped through the door marked Barking Monster and growled, 'A Parson Russell Terrier. A bitch with a pedigree.'

And so it was that I morphed from mild-mannered hack to loony man of letters and became an eye-rolling anecdote: 'What's the worst job you ever had?'

'Getting a small bitch for that AA Gill.'

With a disturbing sense of unreality, I filed the piece on Friday and on Monday a pair of editorial assistants, who presumably had double-firsts from ivy-clad academe and had beaten off hundreds of other applicants to gain a toehold in publishing, presuming that it would be, well, God knows what people presume magazine publishing would be, but certainly not driving to Norfolk and back pretending to be a puppy-less couple on behalf of some columnist with a stratospheric ego crisis.

'It's very sweet,' said one of the young overachievers, 'it's been sick on my lap twice. We called it Biscuit.' Her Biscuit.

'Did you? Can I get you anything? No, well, bye-bye.'

I was beginning to understand why very famous, very mad people are often seen as bad-mannered and distant, and can end up as recluses. It's the look on other people's faces, the shadow of mild disgust insufficiently covered by polite disbelief that exposes the bad behaviour.

So there I was, alone in the house, with a Parson Russell puppy, long-legged, wire-haired, a question mark tail, a tan face with a white blaze. She became Put, the Zulu word for maize porridge. Naming pets is a glimpse into prosaic flights of ego, like the naming of celebrity children. You're not giving the thing an identity; you're putting a label on the new extension of you.

Now I'm not going to give you a long, winsome description of dog and man: the runs through the long grass; the amusing little adventures in the shoe cupboard; the heartache of the worm pills; the crisis of the turd in the early morning kitchen. Humans' stories about dogs come just after their stories about dyspraxic children for their utter hell. Suffice it to say, in language of Californian self-help gurus, I had a dog-shaped hole in my life that Putu filled neatly.

What's always fascinated me is how our species ever got a dog-shaped hole in the first place. Why didn't we have a sloth-shaped hole or a beaver one or a Noah's Ark-shaped hole? I understand this is rather deflecting the subject from my bad behaviour, but actually it's more interesting. Dogs are the oldest of all domesticated animals. Before sheep or cattle, long before horses and arable farming, man shared his hearth and his bones with dogs, and no one knows quite why. The relationship between horses, sheep, chickens and men is obvious. We eat them and sometimes fuck them. With dogs it's not as straightforward. The hominids that walked out of Africa came with dogs at their heels, but why?

The first question that everything in the world asks itself every morning is: 'So, what's in it for me?' It's not clear what was in it for man or dog at the start. Later, of course, dog would herd, guard, catch crooks, find people in earthquakes and be Shep. To see what's in it for the dog, you only have to compare the number of dogs with wolves. Domestication is a vast advantage for a species. The original progenitor of the domestic cow is long extinct. Happily, animals don't have romantic, new-age, green problems with a free life as opposed to a housebound-and-fed life. But in the beginning, the hunter-gatherer and the dog must have been competitors. Packs of dogs would have been after exactly the same food as people and it's safe to imagine that given the opportunity they'd have killed and eaten each other.

Selection and survival are all about opportunity. What the precise set of circumstances was that made dogs and men cohabit we'll never know, but a likely scenario is that a clan of hominids found orphaned puppies. They wouldn't have been an immediate threat, neither would they have been much of a meal. And a human, probably a child, looked at them and went, 'Ah!' And in that instant there was one of those turning points for a species that is the difference between an evolutionary early bath and a seat on the sofa with your own doctor. It was a moment that went into slow motion and had violins as a soundtrack. The dogs recognised the opportunity. This was what dogs had been born for. This was the once-in-a-lifetime opportunity for an entire species.

Hominids and dogs were opportunistic. Most animals made their living by being specialist tradesmen, working to be the most efficient in a particular habitat or circumstance. They play all their evolutionary cards in one hand. But some are generalists, doing a bit of everything, always competing with specialists but able to adapt. It's tougher to begin with, there are a lot of risks and a lot of casualties, but in the end it seems that nature favours the dilettante. Adaptation is the name of the beautiful survival game. And these puppies saw an opportunity. They saw something they couldn't understand, but they saw that they might exploit it. The puppies noticed that humans had a range of expression and behaviour that was outside dog experience but that 'Ah!' showed they could manipulate it. They were the first animals to see and understand the importance of human emotions. To live with men, dogs had to do a pretty swift makeover. You can't have small kids and an adult wolf in the same tent, trust me. So dogs do something called neoteny. They remain in a juvenile state for their whole lives. Domestic dogs grow up to be childish wolves, never getting to adulthood because that would make them unpredictable and violent and a blanket.

Dogs are naturally pack animals so they found it easy to fit in. The biggest problem in becoming domesticated is not for the species who can't live with humans, it's for the ones who can't live with each other. For thousands of years we tried to domesticate cheetahs. They're readily trainable, but you can't breed them because they're solitary. Cheetahs have never managed to get over themselves and now they're endangered. Dogs, on the other hand, now live on every continent and country on earth. They've gone into space, though they didn't know why and they didn't come back. They managed to do one other incredibly clever thing: they mutated faster than any other animal. A new variety can be made in less time than Ferrari can make a new car.

You might say that inventing breeds is wholly human – and choosing the colour swatches and size is – but it can only be managed with the acquiescence of the dog. We've been breeding horses for 3,000 years and a horse is still a horse; there's nothing like the variation between a Chihuahua and a Great Dane. Dog species may come and go but their genes are pooled infinitely.

The first dogs realised that, alone in the natural world, humans crave variety. Everything else wants continuity and certainty, people want novelty. And dogs provided it. What they came up with is the cleverest thing in all of nature: reverse-Darwinism – not the survival of the fittest but the survival of the least fit, the most needy. The Chinese Crested is a completely naked Chihuahua except for a tuft of old man's pubes on its head and tail. It has large, lachrymose eyes, huge ears and a tiny little nose. It feels like dry chamois leather and it'll go floppy in the crook of your arm and stare up at you. It's imitating a human baby. What's even cleverer is that its temperature is a couple of degrees higher than normal. It's imitating a sick baby, so you'll care for it. As an animal, it's a fucking disaster. As a dog, it's supremely successful.

Dogs have understood that they can use their genes to become smaller, furrier, weaker, worse hunters, reedier-voiced. Wolves went on being better and better wolves and now they're just behind the cheetahs in extinction's waiting room.

Dogs, meanwhile, have their own doctors and holiday homes, their own laws, their own human police force (the RSPCA), their own professional association (the Kennel Club) and they have welfare. They live with all the benefits of the most civilised humans. They even have people who follow them round picking up their shit. (This is an utterly inexplicable waste to a dog, but then everything we do is utterly inexplicable to dogs.) They recognise emotion. Over a thousand years they've learned to read it and react to it, but they can have no idea what it means or why we do it. All they know is how to exploit it.

The most fascinating thing about them is that they are no closer to understanding what it is to be human than they were 10,000 years ago, but they pander to our feelings with an infinite subtlety. It's like a play where only half the cast understands the language it's written in. The irrefutable rules of evolution say that there must be something in this relationship for us. And plainly there is: dogs sniff, lead, herd and fetch slippers, but those things don't account for one per cent of dogs. They do something more complex for us. They're nature's yes men. A dog is the ultimate lifetime sycophant. A junkie tramp sitting on a pavement in his own wee can have a dog whose look says, 'You're a god among men.' Dogs allow us to be stars in our own lives. They're an endlessly appreciative audience, our most assiduous fans and obsessive stalkers. It's not for real, of course. They just read us in the way a wolf reads a caribou, and if the caribou had opposable thumbs and a tin opener then the wolf would probably let it get dinner instead of ripping its throat out.

When you fall over and break your hip and can't reach the phone, your dog will try his damnedest to get help. He'll bark and jump and whine and wag. But when no one comes, have no doubts: he'll eat you. He's a dog. In the way of things, when I turned the corner and stepped through the door marked 'Ooh, get you!', and became the monster, God and Darwin (who are an item) had a bit of a laugh and gave me an antidote, brought on the Fool to my Lear.

As I write, Putu's lying on her chair that used to be my chair, and she's watching me. She can watch me for hours and hours. Her expression looks very like devotion. The eyebrows twitch. She rests her chin on her paws in adoration, except she doesn't. Those emotions are exclusively human. What she's doing is learning me. She's reading me like a book. The truth is, I'm the Fool to her Lear. Dogs are bigger and better monsters than we can ever be. They've found the weakness in our huge brains: we're slaves to sentiment and emotions. For dogs, we're just a resource. We're prey.

Virginia Woolf

– *from* Flush: A Biography –

Virginia Woolf (1882–1941) wrote a popular biography of Elizabeth Barrett Browning's spaniel Flush, inspired by the Browning's love letters. Flush led an eventful life: held to ransom by Victorian dog-nappers, and witness to his mistress's secret marriage to the writer Robert Browning. Flush travelled with her from an invalid's room in London's Wimpole Street to Pisa and Florence, doted on by the Brownings. This passage describes Flush's dramatic first encounter with Elizabeth. Flush has come from a life in the country but his mistress has gifted him to her invalid friend.

T hus advancing, thus withdrawing, Flush scarcely heard, save as the distant drone of wind among the tree-tops, the murmur and patter of voices talking. He pursued his investigations, cautiously, nervously, as an explorer in a forest softly advances his foot, uncertain whether that shadow is a lion, or that root a cobra. At last, however, he was aware of huge objects in commotion over him; and, unstrung as he was by the experiences of the past hour, he hid himself, trembling, behind a screen. The voices ceased. A door shut. For one instant he paused, bewildered, unstrung. Then with a pounce as of clawed tigers memory fell upon him. He felt himself alone – deserted. He rushed to the door. It was shut. He pawed, he listened. He heard footsteps descending. He knew them for the familiar footsteps of his mistress. They stopped. But no – on they went, down they went. Miss Mitford was slowly, was heavily, was reluctantly descending the stairs. And as she went, as he heard her footsteps fade, panic seized upon him. Door after door shut in his face as Miss Mitford went downstairs; they shut on freedom; on fields; on hares; on grass; on his adored, his venerated mistress – on the dear old woman who had washed him and beaten him and fed him from her own plate when she had none too much to eat herself – on all he had known of happiness and love and human goodness! There! The front door slammed. He was alone. She had deserted him.

Then such a wave of despair and anguish overwhelmed him, the irrevocableness and implacability of fate so smote him, that he lifted up his head and howled aloud. A voice said 'Flush'. He did not hear it. 'Flush,' it repeated a second time. He started. He had thought himself alone. He turned. Was there something alive in the room with him? Was there something on the sofa? In the wild hope that this being, whatever it was, might open the door, that he might still rush after Miss Mitford and find her – that this was some game of hide-and-seek such as they used to play in the greenhouse at home – Flush darted to the sofa.

'Oh, Flush!' said Miss Barrett. For the first time she looked him in the face. For the first time Flush looked at the lady lying on the sofa.

Each was surprised. Heavy curls hung down on either side of Miss Barrett's face; large bright eyes shone out; a large mouth smiled. Heavy ears hung down on either side of Flush's face; his eyes, too, were large and bright: his mouth was wide. There was a likeness between them. As they gazed at each other each felt: Here am I – and then each felt: But how different! Hers was the pale worn face of an invalid, cut off from air, light, freedom. His was the warm ruddy face of a young animal; instinct with health and energy. Broken asunder, yet made in the same mould, could it be that each completed what was dormant in the other? She might have been – all that; and he – But no. Between them lay the widest gulf that can separate one being from another. She spoke. He was dumb. She was woman; he was dog. Thus closely united, thus immensely divided, they gazed at each other. Then with one bound Flush sprang on to the sofa and laid himself where he was to lie for ever after – on the rug at Miss Barrett's feet.

Lord Byron

– Inscription on the Monument of a Newfoundland Dog –

Poet and politician Lord Byron (1788–1824) had a beloved Newfoundland dog named Boatswain. Byron instructed in a letter to Francis Hodgson of 1808 that Boatswain, whom he had nursed in his dying hours, 'is to be buried in a vault waiting for myself. I have also written an epitaph, which I would send, were it not for two reasons: one is, that it is too long for a letter; and the other, that I hope you will some day read it on the spot where it will be engraved.'

Byron required no epitaph for himself, giving the following instructions in his will: 'I desire that my body may be buried in the vault of the garden of Newstead, without any ceremony or burial-service whatever, and that no inscription, save my name and age, be written on the tomb or tablet; and it is my will that my faithful dog may not be removed from the said vault.'

When some proud son of man returns to earth,
Unknown to Glory, but upheld by Birth,
The sculptor's art exhausts the pomp of woe,
And storied urns record who rest below
When all is done, upon the Tomb is seen
Not what he was, but what he should have been
But the poor Dog, in life the firmest friend,

The first to welcome, foremost to defend,
Whose honest heart is still his Master's own,
Who labours, fights, lives, breathes for him alone,
Unhonour'd falls, unnotic'd all his worth,
Deny'd in heaven the Soul he held on earth:
While Man, vain insect! hopes to be forgiven,
And claims himself a sole exclusive Heaven.
Oh Man! thou feeble tenant of an hour,
Debased by slavery, or corrupt by power,
Who knows thee well must quit thee with disgust,
Degraded mass of animated dust!
Thy love is lust, thy friendship all a cheat,
Thy tongue hypocrisy, thy heart deceit,
By nature vile, ennobled but by name,
Each kindred brute might bid thee blush for shame.
Ye! who behold perchance this simple urn,
Pass on, it honours none you wish to mourn,
To mark a friend's remains these stones arise,
I never knew but one –and here he lies.

Newstead Abbey, October 30, 1808

Chihuahua

David Redmalm

– Holy Bonsai Wolves: Chihuahuas and the Paris Hilton Syndrome –

David Redmalm is an Associate Professor in Sociology and Social Psychology at Mälardalen University, Sweden, and a member of the HumAnimal Group based at Uppsala University, which studies the significance of animals in human lives.

P aris Hilton, heiress of the Hilton hotel chain, was frequently depicted in popular media carrying her favourite dog Tinkerbell Hilton, until the dog passed away in 2015. Tinkerbell's fame, many argued, created an increased demand for Chihuahuas, which in turn resulted in a large number of abandoned Chihuahuas in the United States. This became known as 'the Paris Hilton syndrome.' Chihuahuas clearly suffer from their popularity: several breed-specific Chihuahua shelters and a national Chihuahua rescue group (Chihuahua Rescue & Transport, Inc.) have been created to respond to abandoned, neglected and abused Chihuahuas. But Hilton was not the first person to create a stir around the breed – several 20th century public figures have owned Chihuahuas, including Billie Holiday, Marilyn Monroe and Madonna, and

Chihuahua booms have accompanied the public figures' success. At least in the United States, interest in the Chihuahua breed seems to be less a momentary trend than a fixation that has persisted since the late 19th century.

There is reason to believe that some of Chihuahuas' popularity lies in how they allow contemporary westerners to play with binary oppositions fundamental to their society. First, the Chihuahua undermines the opposition between subject and object, since the Chihuahua is both regarded as a dear companion and as a commodity. Second, the Chihuahua transgresses the boundary between nature and culture, since the dog is both a descendant of the wolf and a social being included in the sphere of human society. While anomalies are often dealt with by means of expulsion, the Chihuahua is instead elevated in a peculiar fashion, both in high and popular culture. The Chihuahua's ambiguity is in some respects reminiscent of the bonsai tree: the dog can be regarded as a piece of nature brought into the social sphere as a portable proof of humanity's omnipotence, thus highlighting what the geographer Yi-Fu Tuan describes as the inseparability of dominance and affection. In short: the Chihuahua is a holy bonsai wolf.

The Chihuahua's transgression of the boundary between nature and culture is also a common theme in western culture, and it is highlighted in historical accounts of the breed. While the Chihuahua is sometimes framed as something unnatural, simply a result of human manipulation, the breed has a much more intricate past. An ancestor of the Chihuahua – the Techichi – was bred in South America for ritual purposes and food as far back as the 9th century in Toltec society, and later by Aztecs. When the Spanish colonized the Mexican region, the Chihuahuas were set free and went to live in the Mexican mountains. The Chihuahua was then re-domesticated and given the name of the Mexican region about 200–300 years ago. The image of the Chihuahua as a hard-boiled survivor, offering dogged resistance in the face of the whims of nature and the constant flux of human societies, thus stands in sharp contrast to the perception of the Chihuahua as a petite fashion accessory.

Several contemporary artists have explored the way the Chihuahua challenges the nature/culture and the commodity/companion binaries. Bjarne Melgaard (1991) performed with live Chihuahuas which he trained to sit still in various poses, highlighting issues of power, socialization and domestication. Scott Musgrove explored the tension between wild wolf and subjugated dog in his depiction of a dreary Chihuahua in a wolf costume, Canis Strategema (2003). In 2007, Daniel Edwards sculpted a diseased Hilton with a grieving Tinkerbell by her side, challenging the traditional sexist association of women with animals, as well as the hierarchical relation between the human owner and the owned animal.

While the image of the Chihuahua as a brittle decorative item is present in handbooks, the breed is described as a 'natural breed', which means that, according to its race specifics, it is not necessary to manipulate the dog's physical appearance. The Chihuahua's long history adds to the perception of the Chihuahua as a real dog with a well-preserved essence: 'As much as they have shaken off their wild vestiges, Chihuahuas still speak the ancestral language of wolves,' Caroline Coile explains in *Chihuahuas*.

In spite of the sometimes cynical observations in Chihuahua manuals, all authors emphasize that it is a constant struggle to maintain a healthy human–dog relationship. Having a Chihuahua is not a guarantee of unconditional love. To earn your Chihuahua's friendship, you have to be sensitive to the Chihuahua's needs and wishes, and as Caroline Coile writes, you have to endure 'the midnight walks in the rain, the soiled floors, the lack of freedom, the expenses […], and ultimately, the grief of parting after a long life.' According to the handbooks, the departure of an individual dog is a tragedy, but the reader is also reminded that there are always new dogs available in the market. The individual/commodity binary even frames authors' discussions of death. A chapter on euthanasia in Ruth Terry's *The New Chihuahua* ends with the dreadful words: 'Enjoy your new Chihuahua!'

After more than a century in the limelight, Chihuahuas have attracted unwanted attention from inept owners and corrupt entrepreneurs. The popular media condemn the objectification and mistreatment of Chihuahuas while westerners simultaneously continue to reproduce an order in which dogs and other animals lack any juridical rights and are regarded as property. Thus, the Chihuahua clearly suffers from the Paris Hilton Syndrome and has a lot to win from its Entzauberung – a demystification of the Chihuahua would make the breed lose some of its appeal. Jean Baudrillard suggests in *Simulacra and Simulation* that animals threaten a universal human identity because they remain silent, no matter how humans treat them. This essay argues quite the opposite – nonhuman animals threaten anthropocentrism in their constant attempts to communicate with humans. Although the handbooks regularly objectify Chihuahuas they also make humans attentive to the way dogs express themselves through body language and sounds. Nevertheless, we humans persist in refusing to take their accounts seriously.

What if one day, all Chihuahuas decided to return to the Mexican mountains, where they lived in peace for centuries? In the movie *Beverly Hills*

Chihuahua, the spoiled Chihuahua Chloe from Beverly Hills gets lost in the desert of the Chihuahua region, but is saved by a group of hundreds of Chihuahuas, living in an Aztec temple. Montezuma, the leader of the group, teaches Chloe about her noble ancestry and why the Chihuahua guerrillas have turned their backs on human society. In his speech, each line is followed by a 'No más!' from the other Chihuahuas:

> We Chihuahuas are not toys or fashion accessories.
> We were not bred to wear silly hats and ride in purses.
> We will no longer be spoken to with baby talk.
> We have been called 'teacup' and 'tiny toy' for too long.
> Names like Fifi, Foo-Foo, Pookie, Pumpkin or Squirt.
> [...]
> Yes, we are tiny, but we are mighty!

J. M. Barrie

– David and Porthos Compared –

In J. M. Barrie's *Peter Pan* Mr Darling requires a nurse
for the children: 'As they were poor, owing to the amount
of milk the children drank, this nurse was a prim Newfoundland dog called Nana, who had belonged to no one
in particular until the Darlings engaged her.' Porthos was
Barrie's first dog, a St Bernard, with whom he walked in
Kensington Gardens and met the children who inspired
his stories. In this extract from *The Little White Bird*,
Barrie imagines writing to a mother comparing Porthos's
character with that of her son David.

I n gentleness David compares ill with Porthos.
For whereas the one shoves and has been
known to kick on slight provocation, the other,
who is noisily hated of all small dogs by reason of
his size, remonstrates not, even when they cling in
froth and fury to his chest, but carries them along
tolerantly until they drop off from fatigue. Again,
David will not unbend when in the company of
babies, expecting them unreasonably to rise to
his level, but contrariwise Porthos, though terrible to tramps, suffers all things of babies, even to
an exploration of his mouth in an attempt to discover what his tongue is like at the other end. The

comings and goings of David are unnoticed by perambulators, which lie in wait for the advent of Porthos. The strong and wicked fear Porthos but no little creature fears him, not the hedgehogs he conveys from place to place in his mouth, nor the sparrows that steal his straw from under him. In proof of which gentleness I adduce his adventure with the rabbit. Having gone for a time to reside in a rabbit country Porthos was elated to discover at last something small that ran from him, and developing at once into an ecstatic sportsman he did pound hotly in pursuit, though always over-shooting the mark by a hundred yards or so and wondering very much what had become of the rabbit. There was a steep path, from the top of which the rabbit suddenly came into view, and the practice of Porthos was to advance up it on tiptoe, turning near the summit to give me a knowing look and then bounding forward. The rabbit here did something tricky with a hole in the ground, but Porthos tore onwards in full faith that the game was being played fairly, and always returned panting and puzzling but glorious. I sometimes shuddered to think of his perplexity should he catch the rabbit, which however was extremely unlikely; nevertheless he did catch it, I know not how, but presume it to have been another than the one of which he was in chase. I found him with it, his brows furrowed in the deepest thought. The rabbit, terrified but uninjured, cowered beneath him. Porthos gave me a happy look and again dropped into a weighty frame of mind. 'What is the next thing one does?' was obviously the puzzle with him, and the position was scarcely less awkward for the rabbit, which several times made a move to end this intolerable suspense. Whereupon Porthos immediately gave it a warning tap with his foot, and again fell to pondering. The strain on me was very great. At last they seemed to hit upon a compromise. Porthos looked over his shoulder very self-consciously, and the rabbit at first slowly and then in a flash withdrew. Porthos pretended to make a search for it, but you cannot think how relieved he looked. He even tried to brazen out his disgrace before me and waved his tail appealingly. But he could not look me in the face, and when he saw that this was what I insisted on he collapsed at my feet and moaned. There were real tears in his eyes, and I was touched, and swore to him that he had done everything a dog could do, and though he knew I was lying he became happy again. For so long as I am pleased with him, ma'am, nothing else greatly matters to Porthos. I told this story to David, having first extracted a promise from him that he would not think the less of Porthos, and now I must demand the same promise of you. Also, an admission that in innocence of heart, for which David has been properly commended, he can nevertheless teach Porthos nothing, but on the contrary may learn much from him.

And now to come to those qualities in which David excels over Porthos – the first is that he is no snob but esteems the girl Irene (pretentiously called his nurse) more than any fine lady, and envies every ragged boy who can hit to leg. Whereas Porthos would have every class keep its place, and though fond of going down into the kitchen, always barks at the top of the stairs for a servile invitation before he graciously descends. Most of the servants in our street have had the loan of him to be photographed with, and I have but now seen him stalking off for that purpose with a proud little housemaid who is looking up to him as if he were a warrior for whom she had paid a shilling. Furthermore, the inventiveness of David is beyond that of Porthos, who cannot play by himself, and knows not even how to take a solitary walk, while David invents playfully all day long. Lastly, when David is discovered of some offence and expresses sorrow therefor, he does that thing no more for a time, but looks about him for other offences, whereas Porthos incontinently repeats his offence, in other words, he again buries his bone in the backyard, and marvels greatly that I know it, although his nose be crusted with earth. Also there is the taking of medicine. For at production of the vial all gaiety suddenly departs from Porthos and he looks the other way, but if I say I have forgotten to have the vial refilled he skips joyfully, yet thinks he still has a right to a chocolate, and when I remarked disparagingly on this to David he looked so shy that there was revealed to me a picture of a certain lady treating him for youthful maladies. Now I refrain from raising hand or voice to Porthos because his great heart is nigh to breaking if he so much as suspects that all is not well between him and me, and having struck him once some years ago never can I forget the shudder which passed through him when he saw it was I who had struck, and I shall strike him, ma'am, no more. But when he is detected in any unseemly act now, it is my stern practice to cane my writing table in his presence, and even this punishment is almost more than he can bear. Wherefore if such chastisement inflicted on David encourages him but to enter upon fresh trespasses (as the girl Irene avers), the reason must be that his heart is not like unto that of the noble Porthos. Thus weighing Porthos with David it were hard to tell which is the worthier. Wherefore do you keep your boy while I keep my dog, and so we shall both be pleased.

Jack London

– *from* The Call of the Wild –

Jack London (1876–1916), was one of the most popular
American novelists and short-story writers of his time.
Born to a working-class unmarried mother, London was
a lifelong socialist. He left school in his teens in search of
adventure and by the age of twenty-two he had worked
on a sealing ship, and followed the gold rush to the
Yukon. In London's novel *White Fang*, the canine hero
makes the transition from wolf to domesticated dog,
while in *The Call of the Wild* the loyal and tireless Buck
reclaims his wolf heritage.

At last, at the end of the fourth day, he pulled
the great moose down. For a day and a night,
he remained by the kill, eating and sleeping, turn
and turn about. Then, rested, refreshed and strong,
he turned his face toward camp and John Thornton.
He broke into the long easy lope, and went on, hour
after hour, never at loss for the tangled way, head-
ing straight home through strange country with a
certitude of direction that put man and his magnetic
needle to shame.

As he held on he became more and more conscious of the new stir in the land. There was life
abroad in it different from the life which had been
there throughout the summer. No longer was this

fact borne in upon him in some subtle, mysterious way. The birds talked of it, the squirrels chattered about it, the very breeze whispered of it. Several times he stopped and drew in the fresh morning air in great sniffs, reading a message which made him leap on with greater speed. He was oppressed with a sense of calamity happening, if it were not calamity already happened; and as he crossed the last watershed and dropped down into the valley toward camp, he proceeded with greater caution.

Three miles away he came upon a fresh trail that sent his neck hair rippling and bristling, it led straight toward camp and John Thornton. Buck hurried on, swiftly and stealthily, every nerve straining and tense, alert to the multitudinous details which told a story – all but the end. His nose gave him a varying description of the passage of the life on the heels of which he was travelling. He remarked the pregnant silence of the forest. The bird life had flitted. The squirrels were in hiding. One only he saw – a sleek gray fellow, flattened against a gray dead limb so that he seemed a part of it, a woody excrescence upon the wood itself.

As Buck slid along with the obscureness of a gliding shadow, his nose was jerked suddenly to the side as though a positive force had gripped and pulled it. He followed the new scent into a thicket and found Nig. He was lying on his side, dead where he had dragged himself, an arrow protruding, head and feathers, from either side of his body.

A hundred yards farther on, Buck came upon one of the sled-dogs Thornton had bought in Dawson. This dog was thrashing about in a death-struggle, directly on the trail, and Buck passed around him without stopping. From the camp came the faint sound of many voices, rising and falling in a sing-song chant. Bellying forward to the edge of the clearing, he found Hans, lying on his face, feathered with arrows like a porcupine. At the same instant Buck peered out where the spruce-bough lodge had been and saw what made his hair leap straight up on his neck and shoulders. A gust of overpowering rage swept over him. He did not know that he growled, but he growled aloud with a terrible ferocity. For the last time in his life he allowed passion to usurp cunning and reason, and it was because of his great love for John Thornton that he lost his head.

The Yeehats were dancing about the wreckage of the spruce-bough lodge when they heard a fearful roaring and saw rushing upon them an animal the like of which they had never seen before. It was Buck, a live hurricane of fury, hurling himself upon them in a frenzy to destroy. He sprang at the foremost man (it was the chief of the Yeehats), ripping the throat wide open till the rent jugular spouted a fountain of blood. He did not pause to worry the victim, but ripped in passing, with the next bound tearing wide the throat of a second man. There was no withstanding him. He plunged about in their very midst, tearing, rending, destroying, in constant and terrific motion which defied the arrows they discharged at him. In fact, so inconceivably rapid were his movements, and so closely were the Indians tangled together, that they shot one another with the arrows; and one young hunter, hurling a spear at Buck in mid air, drove it through the chest of another hunter with such force that the point broke through the skin of the back and stood out beyond. Then a panic seized the Yeehats, and they fled in terror to the woods, proclaiming as they fled the advent of the Evil Spirit.

And truly Buck was the Fiend incarnate, raging at their heels and dragging them down like deer as they raced through the trees. It was a fateful day for the Yeehats. They scattered far and wide over the country, and it was not till a week later that the last of the survivors gathered together in a lower valley and counted their losses. As for Buck, wearying of the pursuit, he returned to the desolated camp. He found Pete where he had been killed in his blankets in the first moment of surprise. Thornton's desperate struggle was fresh-written on the earth, and Buck scented every detail of it down to the edge of a deep pool. By the edge, head and fore feet in the water, lay Skeet, faithful to the last. The pool itself, muddy and discolored from the sluice boxes, effectually hid what it contained, and it contained John

Thornton; for Buck followed his trace into the water, from which no trace led away.

All day Buck brooded by the pool or roamed restlessly about the camp. Death, as a cessation of movement, as a passing out and away from the lives of the living, he knew, and he knew John Thornton was dead. It left a great void in him, somewhat akin to hunger, but a void which ached and ached, and which food could not fill, At times, when he paused to contemplate the carcasses of the Yeehats, he forgot the pain of it; and at such times he was aware of a great pride in himself – a pride greater than any he had yet experienced. He had killed man, the noblest game of all, and he had killed in the face of the law of club and fang. He sniffed the bodies curiously. They had died so easily. It was harder to kill a husky dog than them. They were no match at all, were it not for their arrows and spears and clubs. Thenceforward he would be unafraid of them except when they bore in their hands their arrows, spears, and clubs.

Night came on, and a full moon rose high over the trees into the sky, lighting the land till it lay bathed in ghostly day. And with the coming of the night, brooding and mourning by the pool, Buck became alive to a stirring of the new life in the forest other than that which the Yeehats had made, He stood up, listening and scenting. From far away drifted a faint, sharp yelp, followed by a chorus of similar sharp yelps. As the moments passed the yelps grew closer and louder. Again Buck knew them as things heard in that other world which persisted in his memory. He walked to the centre of the open space and listened. It was the call, the many-noted call, sounding more luringly and compellingly than ever before. And as never before, he was ready to obey. John Thornton was dead. The last tie was broken. Man and the claims of man no longer bound him.

Hunting their living meat, as the Yeehats were hunting it, on the flanks of the migrating moose, the wolf pack had at last crossed over from the land of streams and timber and invaded Buck's valley. Into the clearing where the moonlight streamed, they poured in a silvery flood; and in the centre of the clearing stood Buck, motionless as a statue, waiting their coming. They were awed, so still and large he stood, and a moment's pause fell, till the boldest one leaped straight for him. Like a flash Buck struck, breaking the neck. Then he stood, without movement, as before, the stricken wolf rolling in agony behind him. Three others tried it in sharp succession; and one after the other they drew back, streaming blood from slashed throats or shoulders.

This was sufficient to fling the whole pack forward, pell-mell, crowded together, blocked and confused by its eagerness to pull down the prey. Buck's marvellous quickness and agility stood him in good stead. Pivoting on his hind legs, and snapping and gashing, he was everywhere at once, presenting a front which was apparently unbroken so swiftly did he whirl and guard from side to side. But to prevent them from getting behind him, he was forced back, down past the pool and into the creek bed, till he brought up against a high gravel bank. He worked along to a right angle in the bank which the men had made in the course of mining, and in this angle he came to bay, protected on three sides and with nothing to do but face the front.

And so well did he face it, that at the end of half an hour the wolves drew back discomfited. The tongues of all were out and lolling, the white fangs showing cruelly white in the moonlight. Some were lying down with heads raised and ears pricked forward; others stood on their feet, watching him; and still others were lapping water from the pool. One wolf, long and lean and gray, advanced cautiously, in a friendly manner, and Buck recognized the wild brother with whom he had run for a night and a day. He was whining softly, and, as Buck whined, they touched noses.

Then an old wolf, gaunt and battle-scarred, came forward. Buck writhed his lips into the preliminary of a snarl, but sniffed noses with him, Whereupon the old wolf sat down, pointed nose at the moon, and broke out the long wolf howl. The others sat down and howled. And now the call came to Buck in unmistakable accents. He, too, sat down and howled. This over, he came out of his angle and the pack crowded around him, sniffing in half-friendly, half-savage manner. The leaders lifted the yelp of the pack and sprang away into the woods. The wolves swung in behind, yelping in chorus. And Buck ran with them, side by side with the wild brother, yelping as he ran.

And here may well end the story of Buck. The years were not many when the Yeehats noted a change in the breed of timber wolves; for some were seen with splashes of brown on head and muzzle, and with a rift of white centring down the chest. But more remarkable than this, the Yeehats tell of a Ghost Dog that runs at the head of the pack. They are afraid of this Ghost Dog, for it has cunning greater than they, stealing from their camps in fierce winters, robbing their traps, slaying their dogs, and defying their bravest hunters.

Nay, the tale grows worse. Hunters there are who fail to return to the camp, and hunters there have been whom their tribesmen found with throats slashed cruelly open and with wolf prints about them in the snow greater than the prints of any wolf. Each fall, when the Yeehats follow the movement of the moose, there is a certain valley which they never enter. And women there are who become sad when the word goes over the fire of how the Evil Spirit came to select that valley for an abiding-place.

In the summers there is one visitor, however, to that valley, of which the Yeehats do not know. It is a great, gloriously coated wolf, like, and yet unlike, all other wolves. He crosses alone from the smiling timber land and comes down into an open space among the trees. Here a yellow stream flows from rotted moose-hide sacks and sinks into the ground, with long grasses growing through it and vegetable mould overrunning it and hiding its yellow from the sun; and here he muses for a time, howling once, long and mournfully, ere he departs.

But he is not always alone. When the long winter nights come on and the wolves follow their meat into the lower valleys, he may be seen running at the head of the pack through the pale moonlight or glimmering borealis, leaping gigantic above his fellows, his great throat a-bellow as he sings a song of the younger world, which is the song of the pack.

– Tailpieces –

Dogs are notorious for hope. Dogs believe that this morning, this very morning, may begin a day of fascination, easily grander than any day in the past.
– Donald McCaig

Outside of a dog, a book is man's best friend. Inside of a dog it's too dark to read. – Groucho Marx

Money will buy a pretty good dog, but it won't buy the wag of his tail. – Josh Billings

Be comforted, little dog, thou too in Resurrection shall have a little golden tail. – Martin Luther

I am called a dog because I fawn on those who give me anything, I yelp at those who refuse, and I set my teeth in rascals. – Diogenes

Be the person your dog thinks you are.
– Ricky Gervais

I like animals. If you talk to a dog or a cat, it doesn't tell you to shut up. – Marilyn Monroe

Our perfect companions never have fewer than four feet. – Sidonie Gabrielle Colette

Dogs are the leaders of the planet. If you see two life forms, one of them's making a poop, the other one's carrying it for him, who would you assume is in charge? – Jerry Seinfeld

Free, open love I have looked upon as dog's love. Secret love is, besides, cowardly.
– Mahatma Gandhi

The dog is very smart. He feels sorry for me because I receive so much mail; that's why he tries to bite the mailman. – Albert Einstein

They will wait forever, they love you that much.
– Coco Chanel

PERMISSIONS

Other titles from Notting Hill Editions*

Beneath My Feet: Writers on Walking
Introduced and edited by Duncan Minshull

This anthology rounds up the most memorable walker-writers
from the 1300s to the modern day, from country hikers to
urban strollers. All of them analyse our need to put one foot in
front of the other. Follow in the footsteps of Virginia Woolf,
George Sand, Rebecca Solnit, and many more.

A Twitch Upon the Thread: Writers on Fishing
Introduced and edited by Jon Day

The writers collected here use angling as a way to write about
love, loss, faith, and obsession. As Virginia Woolf observed,
such writing lifts the body 'out of the chair, stands it on the
bank of a river, and strikes it dumb.' Includes contributions
from Charles Dickens, Virginia Woolf, Jerome K. Jerome,
Arthur Ransome, and dozens more.

On Christmas: A Seasonal Anthology
Introduced by Gyles Brandreth

A selection of Christmas-themed writings to savour during
the highs and lows of Christmas Day. Includes selections from
writers old and new, including Dostoevsky, Dickens, A.A.
Milne, C.S. Lewis, and Ali Smith.

On Dolls
Edited by Kenneth Gross

The essays in this collection explore the seriousness of play and
the mysteries of inanimate life. Includes contributions from
Baudelaire, Rilke, Kafka and Freud.

How Shostakovich Changed My Mind
by Stephen Johnson

BBC music broadcaster Stephen Johnson explores the power of
Shostakovich's music during Stalin's reign of terror, and writes
of the healing effect of music on sufferers of mental illness. He
reflects on his own experience, where Shostakovich's music
helped him survive the trials of bipolar disorder.
'Quite simply an essential document' – Tom Service,
Music Matters

Found and Lost: Mittens, Miep and Shovelfuls of Dirt
by Alison Leslie Gold

A memoir from the holocaust writer Alison Leslie Gold, told
through a series of letters. The letters tell of her early activism;
descent into addiction; her fateful meeting with Miep Gies
(the woman who sheltered the Anne Frank family), and her
subsequent recovery.
'Compelling' – *Times Literary Supplement*

What Time Is It?
by John Berger & Selçuk Demirel

A playful meditation on the illusory nature of time by the
visionary thinker John Berger and Turkish artist Selçuk
Demirel. In this beautiful illustrated essay, Berger posits the
idea that by experiencing the extraordinary, we can defy
time itself.

*All titles are available in the UK, and some titles are available
in the rest of the world. For more information please visit www.
nottinghilleditions.com.

A selection of our titles is distributed in the US and Canada by
New York Review Books. For more information on available
titles please visit www.nyrb.com.